SECURE
IN GOD'S
EMBRACE

*Living as the Father's
Adopted Child*

KEN FONG

InterVarsity Press
Downers Grove, Illinois

InterVarsity Press
P.O. Box 1400, Downers Grove, IL 60515-1426
World Wide Web: www.ivpress.com
E-mail: mail@ivpress.com

InterVarsity Press® is the book-publishing division of InterVarsity Christian Fellowship/USA®, a student
movement active on campus at hundreds of universities, colleges and schools of nursing in the United States of
America, and a member movement of the International Fellowship of Evangelical Students. For information
about local and regional activities, write Public Relations Dept., InterVarsity Christian Fellowship/USA, 6400
Schroeder Rd., P.O. Box 7895, Madison, WI 53707-7895, or visit the IVCF website at <www.ivcf.org>.

Scripture quotations, unless otherwise noted, are from the New Revised Standard Version of the Bible,
copyright 1989 by the Division of Christian Education of the National Council of the Churches of Christ in the
USA. Used by permission. All rights reserved.

Photograph used on page 131 is courtesy of Frank Chi.

Cover design: Cindy Kiple

Cover image: Frans Jansen/Getty Images

ISBN 0-8308-2371-9

Printed in the United States of America ∞

Library of Congress Cataloging-in-Publication Data

Fong, Ken Uyeda.
   Secure in God's embrace: living as the Father's adopted child / Ken
Fong
      p. cm.
Includes bibliographical references.
   ISBN 0-8308-2371-9 (pbk.: alk. paper)
   1. Adoption (Theology) 2. God—Love. I. Title.
BT 165.F66 2003
231'.6—dc21
                                                                                          2003010915

P	17	16	15	14	13	12	11	10	9	8	7	6	5	4	3	2	1
Y	15	14	13	12	11	10	09	08	07	06	05	04	03				

To my precious daughter, Janessa

You keep me young, and most of all, you keep giving me new reasons to appreciate the Father's love for his children. I love your kisses!

To my amazing wife, Sharon ("Snoopy")

I can't imagine coming up with more than enough love to lavish on a child with anyone else but you. I love your kisses too!

To Janessa's birth mom

It is only because of your love for Janessa and your courage to go through with the pregnancy that she is alive today and a perpetual miracle to us. She has your intoxicating personality, and she uses it daily to bring joy and laughter to us all. Thank you for entrusting her to us. We will always have room for you in our family because you are one of the most cherished parts of her story. We continue to pray that, someday soon, Janessa's birth dad will want to connect with her too.

To Judie Jue

Thank you for pouring out your abundant love on Janessa and Sharon and me from the very start. In so many ways both big and small you have become a member of our extended family.

CONTENTS

Acknowledgments 9

Introduction 13

1 More Than Enough Love 17

2 To Be Made like God 28

3 Good News for Spiritual Orphans 43

4 A Pre-loved Child 56

5 Full and Forever Family Members 69

6 Drunk with Kisses 85

7 The Only One Worth Loving So Much 99

8 A New Song for a New Family 113

Notes 130

ACKNOWLEDGMENTS

I am grateful this book is finally finished. Just stringing words together isn't that hard. But in moving this book from the initial inspiration through the sermon phase and, finally, to what you now have in your hands, it became amply clear to me that, while putting words down on paper isn't difficult, writing coherently, concisely and comprehensively is extremely painful and arduous. I now have much more respect for those who do this for a living and for those who work behind the scenes to make all of us authors intelligible and accessible.

Every book is the culmination of influential people and events as much as it is an outgrowth of the author's passions and convictions. My book certainly came to be through the contributions and convergence of many different people, but there are some that I feel deserve special acknowledgment.

Thank you, Barney Ford, not just for approaching me for consideration as the Bible expositor for Urbana 2000 but, once I was selected, for giving me permission to tackle this intimidating and auspicious assignment as myself, not as a poor imitation of John Stott! Thank you, too, for the way you prayed for me in your office as I mourned the shocking loss of the baby from Japan.

Thank you, Bob Fryling, for hatching the idea of turning my Urbana messages into a book. You were persistent without putting any pressure on me to get this project done.

And thank you so much to my editors Al Hsu and Cindy Bunch at InterVarsity Press. I honestly dreaded opening the fat packets you sent me because it has never been easy for me to accept criticism lightly. But your questions and suggestions sharpened my thinking and cleaned up my verbiage.

And Joe Stowell, president of Moody Bible Institute, thank you so much for graciously loaning me your only copy of that out-of-print book on ancient adoption laws that proved to be such a crucial piece in my research on Paul's perspectives. You were willing to entrust an irreplaceable book from your library to me even though you hadn't even met me yet.

Thank you, Katherine Bertrand, director of Nightlight Christian Adoptions. If you hadn't been willing to go the extra mile with all of us that Friday in April 1999, we wouldn't have been able to adopt Janessa so quickly. I also must thank adoption attorney David Baum not just for trying to help us find a child in Hawaii but for faxing Katherine the legal forms we needed that crazy day when all of this came together.

I also want to thank my parents, Jim and Emilie Fong, for being such a wonderful example of God's accepting love, especially as you both have genuinely and fully embraced everyone in our family who is adopted or who is not Chinese. Additionally, I'd especially like to thank my adopted niece Kellie for helping me anticipate the special issues that Janessa might face as she gets older.

And thank you so much, Masa and Barbara Samura, for being

inspirational examples to me of the kind of determined love that our Father has for all of us children, no matter what. I want to love our daughter the way you continue to love yours.

Finally, a huge note of gratitude to everyone who is such an essential part of Evergreen Baptist Church of LA, the church I have been called to serve as senior pastor after being on staff here now for over half my life. Thank you for covering for me when I had writing deadlines to meet. Most of all, thank you for helping to turn this metaphor of adoption into a tangible experience of God's unfailing love for all kinds of faith-family members. I love each one of you, and I love being your senior pastor!

INTRODUCTION

I can honestly say that I have never regretted choosing to love God; yet throughout my life as a Christian there have been innumerable moments when I've secretly wondered if my heavenly Father ever regrets choosing to love someone like me.

Having been a part of Christian churches ever since I was a baby, I grew up hearing over and over about God's unconditional love for me, about how special everybody is to the Holy One who created and sustains the universe. In spite of the fact that I was, I am and I will always be an insincere, inconsistent and even, at times, corruptible person, God the Father loved me so much that he sent his innocent and only Son Jesus to come and die in my place. And I was taught that my heavenly Father keeps on loving me, nonstop, in the midst of all my messes and mistakes, to ensure that I will one day reach heaven and rejoice in the rapture of his welcoming presence. From the moment I began to comprehend the profound significance of that timeless Christian message, I knew why they called it the "good news."

For more than two-and-a-half decades I have proclaimed and borne witness to that same great message as a believer, church member, pastor, conference speaker and community leader. But what I have never shared is how, from about fifth grade until I was nearly forty-five years old, I occasionally wondered if God ever had second thoughts about choosing to love and save such a conflicted saint like me. I'm sure that many folks over the years have come to see me as an affable and eager Christian or as a caring and bold pastor, and I've certainly basked in the glow of their warm affirmations. Yet in spite of my positive public persona, I've privately still struggled with secret sins and persistent shortcomings that God knows about full well. My heavenly Father has always had a front-row seat in the melodrama that is my life. God has always been able to see beyond the flattering spotlight into the gloom of my darker self. While this might come as a shock to some, God has always known about my crippling insecurities, my recurring bouts with lust, my refusal at times to forgive, and my struggle to love God, all of my neighbors and especially my enemies—to cite only a few of my ongoing shortcomings. So can you really blame me for losing sleep at times, wondering if my Father is ever so disenchanted with me that he wishes he would have chosen to love someone more sincere, more saintly than I've been all these years and am likely to be as I continue to advance in years?

Does my personal admission of sporadic fear and fretting strike you as odd or out of place coming from a lifelong Christian and a pastor? My guess is that if you've been brutally honest in assessing yourself, you are already well acquainted with this private struggle I've described.

You might be a well-respected and fruitful missionary or maybe a devoted and loving parent. Yet because of covert brokenness or obvious personal flaws there are moments when you secretly wonder if God's love is enough. Or you might be a stellar leader of your campus Christian fellowship or local church, but you too have struggled at times to believe that there truly is nothing that "will be able to separate us from the love of God in Christ Jesus our Lord" because you can readily think of a number of personal failures or flaws that must trouble God mightily (Romans 8:39). If you're not a Christian, you still might not be able to swallow the notion that anyone, let alone a perfect and holy God, would choose to love someone with so many problems. If that's the case, I hope it's strangely comforting to know that a lot more of us Christians share this sense of uneasiness, in spite of appearances to the contrary. But while that certainly was true of me for most of my life, these days I hardly wonder or worry at all that my Father regrets choosing me to love.

Here's what happened. Right before I turned forty-five, I began to appreciate as never before why there really was no basis for my wondering if God ever regrets choosing to love someone as imperfect and sinful as me. At an age and career stage when most of my male peers were sending their kids off to college and perfecting their golf game, I became a first-time father after a prolonged, heart-wrenching adoption ordeal.

The insights my wife and I are gaining about our love for and commitment to our daughter—as we searched the world over for her, as we have made her a member of our family, and as we anticipate her insecurities and the issues that may spring from her adoption—have removed the bulk of my own insecurities about God's love for me because I've been given the opportunity to experience being an adoptive father myself.

This book is a result of coming to grips with what it means to adopt an orphaned, imperfect child and to know that I will love that child forever as nothing less than my very own. To truly understand God's love, you will have to think of yourself as a spiritual orphan and of God as a loving father intent on adopting as many orphaned children as possible into his family. But this book doesn't only contain an oft-overlooked biblical metaphor for salvation. It also contains a very honest account of what my wife and I suffered for nearly four years before we finally were able to adopt our daughter. This is the best way I know to illustrate the power and permanence of the Father's love for each of his adopted children. If at the end you feel more secure in that love and excited about sharing it, or you are open to receiving God's love for the very first time, our experience will be far more meaningful.

MORE THAN ENOUGH LOVE

$\mathcal{D}$o you remember your first kiss? Your first time may not have been particularly pleasant. It may even have occurred under traumatic circumstances, and you'd much rather forget it ever happened. I still remember my first kiss because I was so sure that it was doomed from the outset to be a disaster. We were both fifteen and sophomores in high school. As that defining moment of my early adolescent life was coming to a crescendo, I was internally freaking out. First, I wasn't sure the girl I was about to kiss was as inexperienced as I was. What if she could tell how little I knew? There was no way I was going to confess to her that I'd never kissed a girl before! But even if she was an inexperienced kisser, I was also worried because we both had mouths full of shiny metal braces!

As she closed her eyes and moved her stainless-steel mouth closer to mine, I couldn't help thinking, "The slightest miscalculation and we will shred each other's lips. Even worse, our orthodontia could get intertwined, her parents would find us days later—dehydrated and still locked lip to lip—and then they'd have to call the fire department to apply the jaws of life to separate us!" My first kiss was memorable not because it was so wonderful but because it was so nerve-wracking. Thankfully, I experienced my very first kiss without my worst-case scenarios ever materializing.

Metaphorically speaking, what if I told you that all of us have already experienced that first kiss, but it happened so early in our lives that none of us is able to remember it? I'm not talking about right after you and I were born. Someone no doubt kissed us scant moments after we popped out into the world from the womb— probably our mom, maybe our dad or, if we're adopted, possibly our birth mom. Odds are that someone grabbed hold of our tiny little faces and planted a big wet smooch on our fuzzy little foreheads, welcoming us into the world and into a family. Can you remember that? Of course you can't. Neither can I. But that's still not the first time we were kissed. The first time any of us was kissed was before we were even born.

HOLY KISSES

Understanding what it means to be human and a much-beloved child of God has a great deal to do with how much we understand the importance of kissing. Actually, if you want to get a better handle on what it means to believe in the God of the Bible, then a great place to begin is what some have referred to as the two great kisses in Christian theology.

The first great kiss is the initial kiss none of us can possibly remember, when the awesome God of the universe initializes the brain of every single human being with the sacred breath of life.

The second great kiss is when Jesus, God's only Son, fills the *heart* of every new believer with the breath of new life through the Holy Spirit of God. Each of our lives begins with a holy kiss from our Maker, and every renewed life in Christ begins again with another holy kiss that brings forgiveness of sins, spiritual gifts to build the church and bless others, and a commitment from God our Father to never leave us or forsake us.

Holy kissing apparently was much more a part of the early Christians' lives together than it is today. Drew University's Dr. Leonard Sweet notes that, "In Christianity the kiss had an almost sacramental function from the start. 'Greet one another with a kiss,' Paul says, making it almost into a liturgical observance (2 Corinthians 13:12). Almost all the earliest liturgies of the church mention the kiss. The kiss was a sacred and sacramental sign of love. Not of peace, but of love."[1]

Indeed, for early followers of Jesus, kissing one another must have been a sacred act, an expression of godly love that was quite commonplace. "Greet one another with a kiss of love," says the writer of 1 Peter 5:14. In contrast to numerous contemporary Christian practices, people kissed so much in those first decades of the church that, according to Sweet, Clement of Alexandria complained about those "who do nothing but make the churches resound with a kiss."[2]

Since the New Testament has numerous references to kissing, it's only natural to conclude that kissing carried a great deal of theological significance for the early church. To those of us from modern Western cultures, this must seem quite peculiar, especially since in American culture kissing is reserved for romantic couples, not Christian brothers and sisters. The practice of kissing around the world has not been uniform, and I've heard there are even cultures where virtually all forms of kissing are unknown or taboo. But for the earliest Christians, holy kissing was a frequent practice, probably because it was a tangible expression of what they understood God the Father had done to them. If this was how the Father had expressed love for them, then it was one simple way they would pass that same love to one another.

The theological import of kissing for Jesus and the early church has always been there in full view, if only we have the eyes to see it. The joyful father welcomes his wayward son back home with a huge hug and a big kiss in Luke 15:20. Church members are regularly told to use a kiss to greet one another (Romans 16:16; 1 Corinthians 16:20; 1 Thessalonians 5:26). The unabashedly grateful woman worships a nonplussed Jesus by kissing his feet at a Pharisee's dinner party (Luke 7:37-38). In verse 45 Jesus scolds his host at that party for his insincere and kissless greeting. The self-righteous host refrains from kissing Jesus because only those who are convinced of their unworthiness, yet loved by Jesus, are moved to express their love by kissing the Son of God (Luke 7:45-47). As a result, these kisses are truly holy ones. They are acts of purest love and devotion.

Of course, the one instance of kissing in the New Testament that's familiar even to secular people is the infamous episode in the Garden of Gethsemane. There, Judas Iscariot—one of Jesus' trusted entourage of twelve—identifies him to an armed and angry mob by a prearranged signal: he would give Jesus the customary kiss of greeting, but in actuality it is an unholy kiss of betrayal (Matthew 26:47-49). Jesus is then taken away by the armed and angry mob that had followed Judas and is later tried and executed.

So even here, all the climactic events leading up to Christ's sacrificial death and miraculous resurrection are set in motion by the common practice of kissing, though in this case it was the pseudoholy kiss of a betrayer.

The holy kiss is mentioned seven other times in the New Testament—twice in the Gospel of Luke, and the verb *kiss* is used six times (Matthew 26:49; Mark 14:45; Luke 7:38; 15:20; 22:47). Something significant was going on—something they all understood—and that's why they kept doing it. They practiced holy kissing back then not simply because it was a cultural tradition (and not because they had never heard of sexual harassment laws), but because they were emulating or reenacting what they believed God did to them. Their attitude must have been, "If this is what God has done to us, then we should do it too."

But why did they interpret God's breathing life into them as holy kissing? I've taken at least three classes in CPR (cardiopulmonary resuscitation) in case one of my parishioners or our daughter might suddenly stop breathing. An essential portion of this emergency procedure involves placing your lips on the victim's and breathing into her lungs. Now I could be wrong, but I don't think anyone takes this training because he sees it as a cheap and easy way to steal some kisses. No one in his right mind would ever want to take advantage of an unconscious, non-breathing person. There is nothing remotely romantic about mouth-to-mouth resuscitation because it is performed to save someone from dying. It is in many respects an act of love and perhaps the best illustration of what the early church and the Jews believed happened when the Lord God created human life out of inanimate matter. God took his life-breath and kissed it into something that wasn't alive. Creating us was and is a divine act of *presuscitation*, not resuscitation.

Before the Beginning

Consider what things were like before God decided to create life in the universe. In Psalm 90:2 we find, "Before the mountains were brought forth, or ever you had formed the earth and the world, from everlasting to everlasting you are God." Before the beginning of everything Yahweh God was all there was. There was nothing—no solar systems, no galaxies, no universe—but God. This teaching of the Bible, that the universe is not an eternal entity but was created, came under a great deal of fire in the nineteenth century.

Scientific developments of the twentieth century, however, have pointed even atheistic scientists back to the belief that there was a time when the universe simply did not exist. Today's big bang theory of the beginning of the universe is based on cosmic evidence that it all began some thirteen to seventeen billion years ago. If that is close to the actual age of the universe, it's no wonder that most of us tend to believe that the universe has always existed. But according to Christian astrophysicist Hugh Ross, mounting evidence today continues to underscore the point that while the universe is extremely ancient, like us, it too had a beginning. "New scientific support for the hot big-bang creation event, for the validity of the space-time theorem of general relativity, and for ten-dimensional string theory verifies the Bible's claim for a beginning. In the final decade of the twentieth century, astronomers and physicists have established that all of the matter and energy in the universe, and all of the space-time dimensions within which the matter and energy are distributed, had a beginning in finite time, just as the Bible declares."[3]

While science has needed time to glean the truth about the universe, the Bible has always taught that the universe exists because of a conscious act of God.

Prior to that divine decision, God was all there was, and that was great. Right at the outset the Bible states, "In the beginning when God created the heavens and the earth" (Genesis 1:1). So often I run right past "in the beginning," and I forget that before the beginning there was nothing but God. Truly, God was the only original occupant of all the unimaginable vastness that we now know as our universe. While our Jewish brethren would argue that Yahweh God was alone prior to creating the universe, we Christians believe that this pre-creation Creator was not alone at all. Given our trinitarian bias, when we see the plural pronouns in Genesis 1:26 (emphasis added), "Then God said, 'Let us make humankind in *our* image, according to *our* likeness,'" we presume this is a reference to one God described in the New Testament as existing in three persons—Father, Son, Spirit. Rather than understanding this to be Yahweh God speaking with angelic beings (one traditional Jewish interpretation), we interpret this to be God the Father, God the Son and God the Spirit conversing with each other, deciding to create humankind in *their* likeness.

What I love about this interpretation is that it helps me better appreciate how perfect and wonderful life must have been for God prior to creating the universe and everything in it. Each person of the Godhead knew and loved each other intimately and unconditionally. In John 17:24 when Jesus was speaking of his relationship with the Father, he declared that the Father loved him "before the foundation of the world." This is Jesus' description of what life was like for the Trinity before the universe or anything in it existed.

They didn't need anything. They had each other. They had the perfect intimate relationship with one another. So why create the universe and us?

Here's what we find in the passage, what we find throughout the Bible: no matter how complete or how fulfilling God's existence was prior to creating the universe and us, God longed to create life because God is pure love, and that's what love does. "Whoever does not love does not know God, for God *is* love" (1 John 4:8, emphasis added). There is something about love that must have an object around which to wrap its arms. So even though the Father, the Son and the Spirit lacked absolutely nothing, they apparently were compelled to move beyond loving each other to create life because genuine love keeps looking for opportunities to express itself through things like commitment, nurture, grace, sacrifice and community. I like the way John Ortberg puts it in his book *Everybody's Normal Till You Get to Know Them:*

> God did not create human beings because he was lonely or bored. The religions surrounding Judaism in the Ancient Near East suggested that the gods made human beings to be their lackeys because they needed someone to provide them with food. But the God of the Israelites did not create because he was needy. God created human beings because he was so in love with the community that he wanted a world full of people to share it with. He wanted to invite them all to the dance. And life within the Trinity was to be the pattern for our lives.[4]

The relationship I was in when I experienced my first kiss didn't make it to the end of that school year. However, I did eventually meet someone while I was in seminary, and two years later we were engaged. As our wedding date drew closer, we enrolled in premarital counseling, and one of the questions we asked our counselor was, "How are we supposed to know when it's the right time in our marriage to start bringing kids into this relationship?" And I'll never forget what she told us. She said, "Okay, look. Don't decide to have kids because all your friends are having kids and you're feeling the pressure of getting left behind and off schedule. Don't do it because your relationship with each other has gone stale and you're trying to jumpstart your home life by having someone else to love because you're having trouble loving each other. The time to add another life to your relationship is when you both agree that there is more than enough love between the two of you so that you are eager and able to lavish another life out of your abundance. Knowing when that time is ripe will be more a matter of your hearts than of your heads."

God wouldn't have had any problem understanding when there was more than enough love among the members of the Trinity. And so God created the universe and all of life out of this profound and abundant love they shared. The Godhead's passion was to bring other lives into their circle of life, even if that meant literally complicating their perfect existence by creating the universe with people like us in it.

NOODLES FROM THE GARBAGE DISPOSAL

If you've ever lived alone and you have also shared your space with other living things, then I don't need to tell you that it's much, much easier living by yourself. Whether it's a family member, a roommate or a gerbil, just one other thing living with you can add untold layers of complexity to your life. It's so much simpler when you live by yourself, isn't it? Your life feels pretty complete; your life is already full. You can eat whatever you want to eat, and you can walk around wearing whatever you want to wear (as long as the shades are drawn). You simply don't have all the hassles when you live alone.

When I was in seminary I had three male roommates one year. We had agreed at the outset to share our food and to take turns cooking and cleaning. But that system soon broke down, and the sink and counters were typically strewn with dirty dishes and food in various stages of decay. One evening I walked into the kitchen as one of my roommates was about to rinse some spaghetti noodles. There had been no clean pots to boil the noodles, so my roommate had selected the only available clean vessel—a shallow, Teflon-coated frying pan.

I happened to walk into the kitchen at the precise moment when he had brought the noodles to perfection. He lifted the frying pan from the burner and took it over to the sink to drain away the water. However, there was no cover to that frying pan, so he proceeded to tip the pan slightly under the running water, hoping to remove the water while retaining his noodles. Teflon and slippery noodles have an extremely low coefficient of friction, so I watched as all those noodles went down the garbage disposal. Then, to my horror—he didn't know I was standing there—he reached down into the garbage disposal and pulled out these noodles that were now covered with distorted eggs and rotten peaches (we didn't run the garbage disposal that often). Without hesitating, he washed them off (I use the word *washed* very loosely) under the faucet, put them on his plate and plopped some Ragu on this pile of pasta and pestilence. That was definitely a moment when I felt a direct word from the Lord: "Cook for yourself! Cook for yourself! And it wouldn't be a bad idea to start looking for your own place, either."

Life is clearly much less complicated when you decide not to ask anyone else to share it with you. But as creatures made in God's image, we too have an inner longing for intimacy, to be in significant relationships with those we can love. So we adopt a pet, seek out a roommate, choose a mate or decide to add a child or children to our already crazy lives. From that moment on, our lives become much messier and more complicated, and our friends—especially those who choose to live alone—may question our sanity. But that's also what God did, and that's what many of us will continue to do, in spite of the extra headaches and heartaches. When you have more than enough love, you have to give it away, even as you recognize that your ordered, uncomplicated existence will never be the same.

2

TO BE MADE LIKE GOD

*R*eal and meaningful kisses are often preceded by rich stories of how the love that propels and inspires those kisses came to be. The creation stories found in the beginning of Genesis are ancient, inspired narratives that teach us what God was up to when deciding to make human beings.

CHILD'S PLAY

Creating the universe—an inconceivable undertaking for even those made in God's image—must have been effortless for God, but do you think it was also akin to *child's play* for the Supreme and Only Deity? Assuming that God found great delight in making the first supernova or the very first wombat, is it safe to say that God's level of involvement and enthusiasm was undiminished when making the 44,072nd of the former and the 5,661,835th of the latter? Does restocking the universe ever get mind-numbingly mundane and tedious for God? If my recent experience with our three-year-old is a reflection of the divine imprint on her, then I must believe that God never gets tired of creating more things to tend and lives to love.

When she was almost three, our daughter received a little bottle of bubble solution that we attached to the wall right above the bathtub. Although quite familiar with blowing bubbles using the plastic wand, she was still far from proficient at producing them. After only three failed attempts, her frustration was obvious. This was not fun! That's when it struck me that I could show her how to catch the bubbles that I blew into the air. Her eyes became circles of wonder as she caught that first delicate descending orb on her outstretched wand. Quickly she declared, "Do it again, Daddy!" and, with unbridled delight, she kept repeating this request, discovering different nuances to this fun new game as the bathwater grew colder.

Her interest in this simple game began to diminish a bit after the fourth or fifth time, but creating and filling the universe must have been, and still is, child's play for our Maker. Over and over again, as the Master Designer began filling the cosmos with things that had only before existed in his imagination, God probably gawked with amazement at this latest innovation and then exclaimed, "Let's do it again!" If God's ongoing motivation for creating anything and everything is love in its purest form, then how can we imagine God simply saying, "Let there be this," and "Let there be that," without also appreciating the utter and unabridged joy that must have been behind those simple declarative words.

Sharing this perspective of God as Creator, G. K. Chesterton once wrote, "Grown-up people are not strong enough to exult in monotony. But perhaps God is strong enough to exult in monotony. It is possible that God says every morning, 'Do it again' to the sun; and every evening, 'Do it again' to the moon. It may not be an automatic necessity that makes all daisies alike; it may be that God makes every daisy separately, but has never got tired of making them."[1]

The author of Genesis 1 records that Yahweh God personally spoke everything into being. It was God's own detailed descriptions and dimensions that gave substance and shape to everything that now exists: light and darkness, planets and plants, suns and moons, fish and fowl, creatures of all manner and mode, and ultimately human beings. Everything in the universe is a manifestation of God's infinite creative genius. And after completing it all, "God saw everything that he had made, and indeed, it was very good" (Genesis 1:31). Or to put God's final sentiments in the jargon of some of today's youth, imagine God rapidly pumping a fist up and down and exclaiming, "OH, YEAH!"

Personally choosing to speak every part of creation into existence is yet another indicator of how enthusiastic and involved the Lord God is about everything in the universe. Subcontract this nonstop, repetitive work out to somebody else? God never wanted to delegate any of this then or now, and I don't think it's because of an unhealthy need for control. Some of us imperfect humans might have trouble letting other people in on some of the work we have to do, but that's because we're perfectionists. God is not a control freak. God never delegates the work of creation because he is a master craftsperson; he is an artisan who takes utter delight in every stage of making something out of nothing and in transforming what is common into a one-of-a-kind work of art. It's as if every element in the cosmos has a little tag on it that says, "Handmade by God." As the apostle Paul long ago stated, "For since the creation of the world God's invisible qualities—his eternal power and divine nature—have been clearly seen, being understood from what has been made" (Romans 1:20 NIV).

FEARFULLY AND WONDERFULLY MADE

The invisible qualities—God's eternal power and divine nature—of the unseen Creator are nowhere more in evidence than in every human being. The writer of Psalm 139 stated that every human being comes with a unique and special label: "fearfully and wonderfully made" (verse 14). Everything else may have a tag that says "handmade by God," but imprinted on each and every human soul is something like this: "handmade with extra care and precision by God."

As far as the Bible is concerned, regardless of whether we believe that about ourselves or anybody else in the world, it's still true. The idea that every person is the handiwork of a loving and holy God is one of the fundamental tenets of both Judaism and Christianity. It doesn't matter what you look like or what opinion you hold about the relative value of yourself or others. From God's perspective, the Lord personally made you and every other human being in a unique and wonderful way.

Today there are quite a number of people who are repulsed by this teaching. Instead, they vehemently insist that all living things have the same intrinsic value. And it is true that there are numerous historical examples of how the belief that the human species is the highest form of life has resulted in the senseless destruction or abuse of other life forms on this planet. Some of the most unthinkable atrocities have been committed by groups of people who feel vastly superior to others. But doesn't it seem like a gross overcorrection to assert that killing an insect is the moral equivalent to killing a human being? Believe it or not, that is an example taken right out of the newspaper this year. However well-intentioned animal rights groups like People for the Ethical Treatment of Animals (PETA) are, their position that all of life is equally sacred disintegrates into the dangerous devaluing of human life in order to elevate the value of other life.

Nationally syndicated radio talk show host Dennis Prager, an unbashful practicing Jew, is in the habit of asking his callers how they would respond to this hypothetical question: "If you were standing on the shores of a small lake and discovered that your pet dog and a person you didn't know were both drowning and you could save only one, which one would you save?" What would you do? Most respondents said they would definitely save their dog. When he asked them why they would let the person die instead, they typically said it was because they loved their dog and didn't know the stranger. Some callers were unable to make a choice, but their ambivalence is still disturbing.

The Bible does teach that all of life is sacred because God creates every form of it. However, we must never ignore that God chose to make only humans in his image. As David declared in Psalm 8,

> When I look at your heavens, the work of your fingers,
>   the moon and the stars that you have established;
> what are human beings that you are mindful of them,
>   mortals that you care for them?
> Yet you have made them a little lower than God,
>   and crowned them with glory and honor.
> You have given them dominion over the works of your hands;

you have put all things under their feet,
all sheep and oxen,
    and also the beasts of the field,
the birds of the air, and the fish of the sea,
    whatever passes along the paths of the seas.

O LORD, our Sovereign,
    how majestic is your name in all the earth!
        (Psalm 8:3-9)

Like it or not, this is what the Bible has always taught: God loves us and every other human being far more than God loves the other living things God has created.

Having been a pastor for close to a quarter of a century now, I have had untold occasions where I've had to drive home this message in order to offset a range of dehumanizing points of view. Like when someone asked me to pray with her about being much smaller than most and having to live with the stares and derision. Or when I counseled a devastated couple only days after being told their newborn had Down syndrome. Or the times I've had to teach why refusing to forgive those who've sinned against us multiple times is not an option. Or when I've preached about God's justice for all, including the overlooked. Or when, as a pastor, I feel terribly miscast or unworthy of my role as one of Christ's undershepherds.

In so many instances, coming back to the value that is intrinsic in every person invites us to see them and ourselves through the loving eyes of everyone's Maker. Seeing God's special label enables us to believe that no one—not even an enemy—is less than this: a fearfully and wonderfully wrought gift of God Almighty.

WHAT DOES IT MEAN TO BE MADE LIKE GOD?

While affirming God's handiwork in every person can itself bring about healing, hope and unity, the first two chapters of Genesis contain an even more compelling reason to love God and one's neighbor. To best appreciate this aspect, let's first go back and examine Genesis 1:26 (emphasis added): "Then God said, 'Let *us* make humankind in *our* image, according to *our* likeness." As mentioned already in the first chapter of this book, Christians historically have taken this usage of the first person plural pronouns as God's way of telling us that God is plural. But there are even more instances where the use of *he* or *his* points to the idea that God is singular. In reflecting on this apparent contradiction, Hugh Ross writes: "The basis for this paradoxical use of pronouns is the Hebrew word for God in Genesis 1: *Elohim*. As accurately as we can translate it into English, it means 'the uniplural God.' In other words, God can somehow be simultaneously singular and plural. Here we get our first glimpse of what we later discover to be the Trinity, God's triunity as Father, Son, and Holy Spirit."[2]

So this uniplural God collectively decided to sculpt human beings in *their* image: "So God created humankind in his image, in the image of God he created them, male and female he created them. God blessed them, and God said to them, 'Be fruitful and multiply, and fill the earth and subdue it; and have dominion over the fish of the sea and over the birds of the air and over every living thing that moves upon the earth'" (Genesis 1:27-28). Unlike anything else God formed, the human race—us, every one of us, every person in this world—is created in God's image. We resemble our Creator.

In his compelling book *The Genesis Question*, Ross states that to be human essentially involves having the following unique characteristics:

- awareness of a moral code "written" or impressed within a conscience

- concerns about death and life after death

- propensity to worship and desire to communicate with a higher being

- consciousness of self

- drive to discover and capacity to recognize truth and absolutes[3]

Awareness of a moral code "written" or impressed within a conscience. Because each of us is crafted in God's image, each person is "hard-wired at the factory" to know the difference between right and wrong, to be capable of feeling appropriate guilt. Even though rampant relativism today makes it seem like most people are missing this inborn ability, the truth remains that the code is there.

For instance, the same person who usually promotes being tolerant of all manner of offbeat or immoral behavior (except for embracing evangelical Christian beliefs) would be outraged if a drunk driver struck and killed her only child. Or if I simply decided to take possession of your three-hundred-dollar fountain pen, even if I believed this was not stealing, you would be really upset. People today are tolerant only of actions or beliefs that don't really impact their own circles of life. However, when things do cross that personal line, everyone's uniquely human, godlike ability to discern the difference between right and wrong kicks in immediately.

Concerns about death and life after death. Being made like God also means that, unlike anything else in all creation, we are aware of not only our own existence but our looming nonexistence. Although all living things must eventually die, having a higher self-consciousness means that we alone must dwell in the shadow of our mortality. Think of the difference between your life and a dog's. I'm not sure either of our two retrievers is glad to be alive, and I'm positive they don't spend one ounce of mental or emotional energy fretting that their life spans will average only twelve human years. While appearing intelligent and displaying a range of emotions, both dogs simply appear to exist without ever contemplating their existence. When we're younger, we almost display a similar tendency to live in blissful ignorance of our inevitable limitations. However, if a child is exposed to a great deal of pain and suffering, the child has a far greater likelihood of worrying about sickness and death.

Much of Western culture, even within sizable pockets of Christianity, tries to shield us from the limitations of aging and the specter of death. For the first forty years of my life, I felt as if I were going to be vital and alive forever. Having passed the midway portion of my own existence now, I find myself much more aware that I'm heading for a definite appointment with my own demise. This profound midlife awakening increasingly rouses me to savor whatever moments I have now of health and bliss, for every day I am moving closer to the time when good health, at least, will be the exception rather than the rule.

Growing older and ever closer to death also intensifies my appreciation for my promised salvation to an eternal life through Christ Jesus far more than years of studying the Bible, preaching about the topic or even presiding over funerals has ever accomplished. An outcome of being made in God's image is, at some point, to face head-on the simple fact that each of us must die someday. Some may see God's giving us this death-consciousness as a curse and would much prefer the naïve life of a dog or a trout. But you can really come to view it as a blessing from God. Only God and those made most like God innately know that life is a transient gift, one that must be both cherished and invested wisely, for each person's time on earth will run out soon enough. Throughout history, this growing sense of urgency has been the motivation for otherwise distracted people to pursue passions and to probe for what waits just beyond death's door.

Propensity to worship and desire to communicate with a higher being. All human beings have a propensity to worship. That too comes with being the only ones made most like our Maker. Our primeval predecessors worshiped whatever they believed was responsible for their well-being: volcanoes, the sun, mythical creatures and unseen suprahuman beings. History has shown that we humans are the only species to look beyond ourselves for a higher power, to believe in a god or deities that far surpass our mortal limits. God's creating us in "their" image has meant from the very beginning that humans have emerged in this world with an instinctive urge to worship the One we believe to be responsible for all of this.

When we're babies, we think our parents are God. But that notion usually fizzles out sometime before puberty strikes, and by then we've probably transferred our worship to the high school heartthrob or some larger-than-life celebrity. During young adulthood, many of us come to worship ideas or ideals, but once we become adults we often resort to worshiping what we feel brings us the most security and happiness: our enormous new SUV, our spacious home in a great school district, our precious and maybe even precocious children. We can even worship our religion for the comfort it apparently provides.

But God didn't instill within each of us this unquenchable desire to worship only to see it spent on anything other than the Lord God alone. According to the Bible, to shower our love and loyalty on something that doesn't deserve it is called idolatry. "Do not be afraid," Samuel told the people of Israel. "You have done all this evil; yet do not turn away from the LORD, but serve the LORD with all your heart. Do not turn away after useless idols. They can do you no good, nor can they rescue you, because they are useless" (1 Samuel 12:20-21 NIV).

In his delightful little book *Wishful Thinking* Frederick Buechner writes, "Idolatry is the practice of ascribing absolute value to things of relative worth. Under certain circumstances money, patriotism, sexual freedom, moral principles, family loyalty, physical health, social or intellectual preeminence, and so on are fine things to have around, but to make them the standard by which all other values are measured, to make them your masters, to look to them to justify your life and save your soul is sheerest folly. They just aren't up to it."[4]

Consciousness of self. A fourth trait that the Lord imparted to make us uniquely like God is, ironically, often what holds us back from freely worshiping God: our intense self-awareness.

I can recall how, back in the mid-'80s, what was then known as the "charismatic renewal" was influencing our church's worship times. Here I was, part of a historic noncharismatic American Baptist church and having roots in a culture not known for being overtly demonstrative in public, with an alarming number of folks around me starting to close their eyes and lift their hands and face toward heaven as they sang.

Conspicuous in those days because of my place on the dais up front, I can still remember inwardly battling my desire to worship God more expressively yet worrying about what other people might think if they saw me letting go of my inhibitions. Eventually, I came to realize that being that self-conscious is pretty much the antithesis to worshiping God. If you're still fretting about some awful headline or are distracted by a doctor's diagnosis, or if you're simply anticipating going out to lunch with friends following the benediction, you're too wrapped up in yourself to get all wrapped up in the presence of the holy God. Worrying more about what God is thinking of you than what others might be thinking of you will push you to lose yourself in the process of rediscovering your Maker, Lord and Savior. As Buechner remarks, "A Quaker Meeting, a Pontifical High Mass, the Family Service at First Presbyterian, a Holy Roller Happening— unless there is an element of joy and foolishness in the proceedings, the time would be better spent doing something useful."[5]

If being so self-aware is an impediment to the unabashed worship of God, then why do you suppose God specifically gave us this godlike attribute? My own experience makes me believe that the Lord made us conscious of who we are because this is how we can realize that, on our own, we are spiritually destitute and alone. Without this divinely prescribed ability, we might never discover that we are all spiritual orphans in need of a father and a family. Allowed to go in one direction, we become too self-absorbed, vain and conceited. However, if our self-awareness is encouraged to expand as God desires, we may find ourselves on the path of self-denial, commitment and giving that Jesus has already trod.

Drive to discover and capacity to recognize truth and absolutes. The remaining distinguishing characteristic is that the Lord made us all naturally inquisitive. We typically enjoy learning and especially want to discover more about the cosmos and our distinct place in it. In this regard, we all are truly like those who at some age learn they are adopted. Even if we have a loving family and a distinct place in the world, finding out that our origin predated all of what has been so familiar both intrigues and mystifies us. Where possible, we want to know who gave us this gift of life, how they felt about us then and, if possible, now. And like nearly every adopted child, we all privately entertain fantasies about one day enjoying a close relationship with the ones whose image we carry in our genes and in our souls.

Although this is a common fantasy among actual adoptees, some who locate their birth parents are rejected by them. What a blow it must be to search and search for them, only to be told that they do not share your desire for a relationship of any kind. But the Bible says those who embark on a search for the One who made them and whose image they carry will not be disappointed:

- "But if from there you seek the LORD your God, you will find him if you look for him with all your heart and with all your soul" (Deuteronomy 4:29 NIV).

- "A father to the fatherless, a defender of widows, is God in his holy dwelling. God sets the lonely in families" (Psalm 68:5-6 NIV).

- "He is the father of all who believe" (Romans 4:11 NIV).

Why does God want to be found by us, and why does the Lord promise to father us when we do find him? The answers to those two questions are best understood if we zoom in for a close-up of that first great kiss in Christian theology: when the Lord God first breathed life into those made most like himself. "The LORD God formed the man from the dust of the ground and breathed into his nostrils the breath of life, and the man became a living being" (Genesis 2:7 NIV).

CREATED IN INTIMACY FOR INTIMACY

Do you remember the CPR example from the first chapter? The image here in Genesis of God breathing life into Adam through his nostrils reminds me of how I was taught to perform cardiopulmonary resuscitation on an infant or small child. When the lifeless person is much smaller than the one administering CPR, you place your mouth over both his mouth and nostrils before breathing deeply into his lungs. Reconsidering this scene from Genesis as one where the infinite Lord is kissing Adam tenderly to life conveys much more of the intimacy of that moment than the literal image of God only blowing into Adam's nose to animate him.

Believing we were created *in* intimacy should make it easier for us to believe that God created us *for* intimacy with him. The Lord created us because the uniplural God had more than enough love, and so the Lord lovingly and painstakingly crafted us in our mother's wombs, kissing us into existence. And I'm convinced the main reason God chose to make us most like himself—conscious of who we are, longing for relationship and with a desire to know the Truth—is so all of us would grow up with this mysterious yearning or longing inside to find our Creator and to enjoy an intimate relationship with him.

This inbred desire on all our parts to love God is actually a response to God's loving us first. In 1 John 4:19 it says, "We love because he first loved us." Therefore, we shouldn't be afraid of God rejecting our love, because as the One who loved us first, God longs for the day when as many of his orphaned children as possible will find him and return his love. When we worship God, that's what we're doing—responding to God's love by loving the Lord back. You might find it fascinating that one of the Greek words for worship, *proskyneō,* literally means "to kiss toward." Worship, then, is when we learn to return God's kisses with kisses of our own.

From the first moment we welcomed our daughter Janessa into our family, I've been kissing her. On her little forehead, on her rosy cheeks, even on her lips (not very Asian of me). Thus far there hasn't been a single day when I've been home that I haven't kissed her and told her how much I love her. But for the longest time, mine were one-way kisses. All she did was receive her daddy's kisses. And that was fine with me, because my kisses were not given to make her kiss me back. They were simply expressions of my unbounded love for her. But on August 31, 2000, Janessa kissed me back for the first time! As I was thrilling to the thought that our sixteen-month-old was beginning to love me back, I concluded that she was merely mimicking what she saw the big purple dinosaur Barney do on television. Nevertheless, I still cherish that first kiss from her because it signaled the beginning of a shared and intimate relationship between a father and a child.

That first little peck on my lips had been preceded by hundreds of unconditional kisses from me. If she grew up never kissing me back, I would have accepted that, but it wouldn't have been what I longed to see happen. But now I can well imagine how thrilled our Father God will surely be when saints from every tribe, language, people group and nation finally return *his* divine kisses.

3

GOOD NEWS FOR
SPIRITUAL ORPHANS

So the first one ever to kiss us was God our heavenly Father when he lovingly and tenderly breathed his own life into each of us. Whether or not we've been aware of it, it's been God's daily, unmerited kisses that have given us everything we've required to keep us alive and growing: the blessing of needed resources, the gift of consciousness and myriad opportunities to grow in wisdom and maturity, a fresh perspective on difficult situations, the daily invitation to spend time with those we love and our heavenly Father. It has always been God's hope that soon all of those made most like God will one day want to return those kisses, worshiping the Lord with unbridled gratitude.

But from a human perspective, our heavenly Father has a huge dilemma. None of us is capable of remembering God first kissing us alive, so is it any wonder that so few are inspired to kiss God back? This might even include numerous professed Christians who nevertheless sit there each Sunday, aloof and unmoved throughout the worship service, demonstrating that it's possible to embrace faith in God without feeling embraced by the object of that faith! In defense of this widespread apathy and amnesia, if none of us can remember when our parents first kissed us, how can we be expected to remember being kissed before we were even born, before we even had consciousness? If God hopes for us to one day gratefully return his kisses, this could be quite problematic.

To complicate things further, this whole subject of holy kissing can be difficult for some of us given the experiences we've had being kissed by other people. We might have grown up believing that no one has ever really kissed us without wanting something in return. Or maybe we have never felt truly worthy of unconditional kisses. Has it ever felt as if people loved you because they have more than enough love to share?

People may kiss us in order to get something from us. They may have a deep need rooted in their own deficient love and actually may want to get some expression of love from us. Though the closeness and intimate contact might be quite enjoyable initially, eventually our souls know that the kiss is an act of taking rather than giving, a feigned expression of affection that may secretly want to possess or control, not bless and endow. Only God the Father's kisses can always be an exhalation of blessing, an unconditional gift of life and love.

UNLOVED AND UNWANTED

Referring to ourselves as sinners or the sinned against certainly describes a significant aspect of our dilemma, but those two labels don't address the profound sense of being unloved and un-wanted. Yes, many of us are painfully aware that we're unholy, unreliable and maybe even unbearable sinners. Or perhaps we see ourselves more readily as the sinned against, hapless victims of other people's cruelties or shortcomings. Clearly the gross identification one way or another with the consequences of sin—our own and others—is one of the most vital ways to connect with our universal need for Jesus and his selfless sacrifice on the cross more than two thousand years ago.

Restraining our self-understanding only to what sin is capable of avoids an oft-overlooked element of our humanity that is grounded in the essence of God's creating us and in our sense of place in this world. The word *orphan* construes this distinctly re-lational component of our spiritual condition.

We typically understand an orphan to be a child who has been deprived, by death or circumstance, of one or both parents. It's a label that is typically draped with sadness, especially when the or-phan is a baby or a young child. The thought of children having to grow up and find their place in the world without the benefit of parents can make us all feel bad. Children are supposed to feel safe and secure because their parents love them and will always be there to watch over them. To have to grow up without parents means to fend for yourself, to have to fight for everything alone, maybe even to survive in a foster home or an orphanage.

That traditional understanding of being an orphan doesn't ap-ply to most of us. If our parents raised us, we have no clue what it would be like to grow up without them. Still, I believe that to some degree all of us will eventually be able to identify with an essential aspect of being orphans ourselves. The odds are that you will outlive your parents. If that happens, on the day you lay the remains of the last one in the ground, you will doubtless suddenly feel like an orphan, too, alone in the world for the first time in your life because you no longer have any parents. The emotions attached to that milestone may soon fade into the background of our adult lives, but at some point, nearly all of us will be able to identify with so forlorn a term as *orphan*.

Did you know that a person can grow up with loving parents, yet still on some level feel like an orphan, unsure at times of his place in the world? Anyone who's been placed for adoption by birth parents, even if the adoptive parents are loving and generous, knows what it's like to struggle with feelings of being unwanted or insecure. Why didn't my birth parents want to keep me? Do they wonder about me and how I've turned out? Would they ever want to meet me someday? How would my adoptive parents feel if I asked to look for my birth parents? Do my adoptive parents ever wish they hadn't picked me? If they had to do it all over again, would they still choose me, even with the trouble I've caused them? And in the case of an international adoption: Why wasn't there at least one relative who wanted to keep me in the family instead of sending me halfway around the world, causing me to lose my native language and heritage and setting me up to feel so different all the time? These are only some of the thoughts that can percolate through the minds of children even though they might have been placed in great homes. Part of them still can identify with feeling like an orphan, like there's still something empty inside, something missing.

I've known a number of adult adoptees who still secretly struggle with core identity and attachment issues. They'd been born in

Asia but were adopted by American families, many of whom were Caucasian. Having been abandoned shortly after birth and initially raised in orphanages, some enjoyed intact families while others weathered divorces and even the premature deaths of parents. They ask, "How can I ever make a commitment to someone in the future if I am still haunted by nagging questions tied either to my unexplained beginnings or the unfortunate uncertainty of my fractured family?"

Spiritually speaking, each of our souls can resonate on some level with the inner angst of these former orphans. If we are really honest and reflective, we too will admit to having lingering questions about our true origins, about the ultimate meaning of our life or about where we truly belong, and these are questions without ready answers.

THE WAY HOME

In James 1:27, the apostle says, "Religion that is pure and undefiled before God, the Father, is this: to care for orphans and widows in their distress, and to keep oneself unstained by the world." Apostle James's widows-and-orphans-based description of undefiled religion shows that God has a very special place in his heart for those who feel estranged or alone in the world. Our heavenly Father is concerned with making everyone feel loved and welcomed into God's household of faith, even strangers or outsiders. "So then you are no longer strangers and aliens, but you are citizens with the saints and also members of the household of God" (Ephesians 2:19). If God cares this much for literal orphans, doesn't it follow that he cares for spiritual orphans as well?

If you can relate to feeling at times like a spiritual orphan—

unloved and unwanted—then I pray that you are brimming with hope to hear that there is a Father who loves you so much that he is always looking for you and your orphaned spiritual siblings in order to bring back as many as possible into an intimate, wonderful, worshipful relationship with himself. The Bible teaches that this heavenly Father loves us all so much that he sent his own Son Jesus to earth to be both the messenger and the means of real hope and redemption. "God's love was revealed among us in this way: God sent his only Son into the world so that we might live through him. In this is love, not that we loved God but that he loved us and sent his Son to be the atoning sacrifice for our sins" (1 John 4:9-10). Jesus' death and resurrection not only made forgiving our sins possible, but it also provided the only means for any of us to come home to God's forever family.

God the Father initiated both our salvation and our reunion by loving us first. God has never forgotten or abandoned all those he has kissed with his own breath of life, be they Jew or Gentile, slave or free, male or female. Through Jesus and his Spirit, God the Father pursues every spiritual orphan in an effort to invite each one to come home to the One who first kissed them.

Three days after Jesus died to remedy our sins and restore the way home to the Father, he came back to life. This was as he had predicted throughout the previous three years of his earthly ministry in the region around the Sea of Galilee in Israel. Since God's divine Son had chosen to come to earth as a Jew in Israel, his initial audience and entourage were overwhelmingly Jewish, as were nearly all the first converts to his "form" of Judaism. But this real hope was ultimately for all who felt unloved and unwanted, not only those who were Jews. So, shortly after Jesus ascended into heaven, he commissioned someone to extend that invitation beyond the Jewish circle. He selected Saul, a bicultural, seminary-trained Jew, himself a product of Jewish migration over the years to the area known then as Asia Minor.

On a grimy road outside of Damascus, the risen Jesus confronted a chastened and chagrined Saul, whom he later renamed Paul (Acts 13). That new Greek moniker would serve Paul well since Jesus was calling him to be the first missionary to the mainly Greek-speaking and Greek-cultured Gentiles in his familiar stomping grounds, far from the place Jesus had selected as the beachhead for his mission to save our lost world. What we know as the book of Ephesians is one of the extant letters that the apostle Paul wrote to first century converts in what are now places like Greece and Turkey.

Ephesians begins with Paul identifying himself to his readers. While it is the custom today for the sender to sign his or her name at the end of a letter, writers of letters in ancient times did the opposite. This was because they used rolled up scrolls, which would have made it difficult to determine the identity of the sender if he had waited to sign it at the end. This writer was well known to his audience, a Jewish lawyer who had trained as a Pharisee, a zealous persecutor of those he originally believed to be aberrant Jews, one who was saved on the Damascus road by the risen Christ to spread the good news about Jesus far beyond the Jewish cultural and racial circles. Here in Ephesians 1:1, Paul understands that the rest of his life has been totally redefined by this saving act of Christ: "Paul, an apostle of Christ Jesus by the will of God."

God's amazing love had kept pursuing him, even though he believed he already knew God thoroughly, and in spite of the fact

that he had been working tirelessly and violently to curtail this
cult that had sprung up after the execution of what he believed to
be an uneducated, itinerant rabbi from some backwater nowhere.
His becoming the first evangelist and church planter among the
Gentiles was no random decision or self-inspired career change,
not something that he simply chose to do. If asked, he might have
explained, "My sincere repenting of my brutal and relentless pursuit of Christians is the result of God's relentless pursuit of me, the
worst of sinners and a lost soul. It is literally by the grace and will
of God that I am the person that you all now know and love" (1
Timothy 1:12-17, paraphrase). In referring to his salvation as
"God's will," I believe a grateful Paul was not simply describing
God's ultimate *plan* for him, but he was also crediting his heavenly
Father's *determined love* for finally finding him and declaring him
to be a valued member of God's family and its first ambassador to
Gentile orphans.

A DETERMINED LOVE

We often limit our understanding of "God's will" to mean the
Lord's divine plan or purpose when it could also point to his
dogged determination to see something happen. For example, after an initial false start more than fourteen years ago, I decided in
1997 that I was definitely going to learn to play golf. Five years
later, I was still flailing away at that unflinching target, which was
an outcome of both my *purpose* and my fierce *determination* to
keep learning this frustrating game in the face of limited opportunities to play and my lack of much natural ability. *Will* implies
both a definite *plan* and a determined *pursuit*. While you may already know a great deal about God's plan to give spiritual orphans

a home and a family, I'm guessing that you don't know that much about how determined this loving God is to find and love as many as possible. God's determination to find us and love us plays a huge part in our becoming children in God's family.

Ephesians 1:1 addresses the recipients: "To the saints who are at Ephesus and are faithful in Christ Jesus." Paul was writing to early converts in a very strategic metropolitan port. Apparently these Ephesian Christians were known far and wide. In verse 15, Paul exclaims, "I have heard of your faith in the Lord Jesus and your love for all the saints." Paul was writing to earnest Christians, folks whom God had already "found" who not only unashamedly loved Jesus but who had more than enough love to bless their fellow followers. People in sister churches throughout that vast region had all heard about them through word of mouth as well as through the recitation of circulating letters like this one.

Following the apostle's opening greeting Paul issues a detailed theological explanation for God's determination to find us and love us (Ephesians 1:3-14). This is what is known as a *doxology*, a declaration of praise for God that poured out of Paul's grateful heart and mind. In this outpouring of thanksgiving, Paul offers up his worship to the Lord: "Blessed be the God and Father of our Lord Jesus Christ, who has blessed us in Christ with every spiritual blessing in the heavenly places" (Ephesians 1:3). Paul strongly believed that each of us should be blessing God as an unending act of gratitude for all the blessings the Lord continues to pour out on us.

Paul hits on an essential truth: the degree to which we actually bless God (and others) is tied to how much we feel God has blessed us. If you ever feel inhibited or limited in your ability to express your love for God—referred to earlier as "kissing God back" and "worshiping the Lord"—not only in a worship setting but also with your entire life, your natural response is directly related to how much you've really identified and appreciated how much God has first blessed you.

If you're not feeling blessed or grateful, it's hard to bless somebody else or demonstrate any real gratitude. In Luke 7, the party crasher blessed Jesus by loving him unashamedly in front of a scandalized host because she had had an earlier experience of his forgiving love. She bathed and kissed Jesus' feet because she had already received more than enough love from him. Her heartfelt blessing of God's Son flowed naturally out of a new inner storehouse of abundant blessing from Christ Jesus. The host of the dinner party, in spite of all his outward trappings, failed to bless the Son of God because his sense of self-righteousness caused him to believe he had no need for Jesus' blessings of forgiveness and grace. As a result, it literally wasn't "in him" to bless Jesus or anyone else, for that matter.

In our church we sometimes talk about scarcity and abundance as indicators of our real spiritual condition. When you're feeling abundant you can freely pass out compliments and truly rejoice in other people's endeavors and successes, but when you're feeling scarce inside, not grateful, and someone gets an award, you think, "That's one less award for me," right? Or someone gets a girlfriend or boyfriend, and a voice inside you says, "That's one less person that might love me." Examples of inner scarcity abound. The whole awful sense of ingratitude makes it hard to be joy-filled and to bless other people. The apostle Paul is saying, in a spiritual sense, that this same thing is going on; if we are not yet deeply aware of every spiritual blessing God has poured out on us, we—

no matter how much we want to try to worship God—are going to have problems returning that love because we're not feeling unbelievably blessed by the Lord.

UNBELIEVABLY BLESSED

Some of you must be thinking, "If God has poured out a boatload of blessings on me, why don't I feel that blessed? How come I feel more like I've been cursed, that God has chosen to withhold his blessings rather than dole them out? Look at my life, where I've come from, what my family or my people have had to endure. How does that make me blessed, not merely with a modest blessing but with *every* spiritual blessing? So excuse me if I have trouble blessing God because I don't feel like God has blessed me; he's messed with me."

Not long ago, some very wealthy people we know adopted a little eight-month-old girl from China. They came back with this tiny baby, plucked from an austere orphanage and a life of certain poverty and disenfranchisement. This baby girl was rescued from an orphanage in China and hasn't a clue what has happened to her. It was like her new parents simply walked into the orphanage and proclaimed in a bold voice, "Who wants to be a millionaire? This is not a game. This is very real. You don't have to answer any questions; all you have to do is become our daughter. Receive our love and care and, hopefully, one day soon, love us back."

And on what otherwise was an ordinary day, out of the hundreds of orphaned little girls, one was picked and immediately transported from a life of poverty to the lap of luxury, from an orphanage in China to the yacht club in Southern California, from being utterly alone and unwanted to feeling much sought after and incredibly special.

A short while later I happened to be with my niece, who was then a college freshman. Since she too had been adopted as a very young child (but from Korea), I wanted to know what she thought about this little girl's incredible good fortune. I remarked, "What do you think about this? It's as if this little girl from China won the lottery, and she doesn't have a clue."

My niece caught me off-guard with her immediate reaction: "You know what? I feel the same way."

I replied, "But your dad and mom weren't millionaires. And your life growing up has been far from easy, right? So how can you say that you feel as incredibly blessed as that Chinese baby?"

She simply said, "Because I was chosen too. Maybe not by millionaires, but at least by two people who wanted me to be their daughter, wanted to love me as part of their family. No matter how hard my life is I am so grateful that my adoptive parents found me and blessed me with a much better life than I would have had if I'd grown up in that orphanage in Korea."

Do you ever feel grateful like that? The Bible says that no matter how messed up our lives might be and how we might have contributed to the mess, there's something that God has done, something that has left us with every spiritual blessing. Paul was reminding his constituents of this when he wrote: "He chose us in Christ before the foundation of the world to be holy and blameless before him in love" (Ephesians 1:4).

Our complete spiritual blessing is this: before he created this world, God already determined to love us. God chose to pursue us, to look for us even if we didn't want to be found. And when he finds us, God joyfully wraps us into his forever family, making us holy and blameless even though we are corrupt and liable. Even though it's easy to believe that being adopted by a wealthy couple is to be blessed in every possible way, there are numerous examples of how children from rich families grow up spoiled and even self-destructive. While living in the lap of luxury can be much more a curse than a blessing, living in the ever-deepening experience of God's unwavering love can only be an indescribable wonder.

4

A PRE-LOVED CHILD

*P*aul correctly noted that the means of the Father's amazing love is none other than Jesus, God's only Son. It was his willingness to suffer the penalty for our sins that proved how much Jesus truly loves us. His resurrection back to life on Easter established that, as he had claimed, he was in fact the Christ, the Greek version of what the Jews call Messiah or Savior. Only God's Son, holy and blameless, could secure for us the hope of being the Father's adopted children. Jesus' willingness to die in each of our places is the most telling example of how determined the Lord God is to love us back into his arms.

Jesus died for us because he is part of the celestial Trinity that chose to love us "before the foundation of the world" (Ephesians 1:4). Coming to earth as a human being and sacrificing his own comfort and life were all essential steps in Jesus' own determination and commitment to love us. This divine choosing is commonly known as *election*, which typically states that though all humans are sinful and deserving of nothing but harsh judgment and eternal punishment, God mysteriously elects to save some because of his mercy and grace. Keeping this in mind, let me introduce a word that captures the whole concept of election in a more relational way, one that focuses less on us knowing exactly whom God has selected and more on how wonderful it is to be ones so special to God.

In 1999 the *Encarta World English Dictionary* contained a brand new word that originated in New Zealand and Australia: *pre-love*. In Los Angeles, when you go to the west side and drive by expensive car lots, they claim they're not selling any used cars. Instead, they offer *pre-owned* cars. But the Australians and New Zealanders haven't sold pre-owned cars for years; they're selling *pre-loved* vehicles. I'm not sure would-be buyers in these two countries trust this marketing ploy, but the concept nevertheless has great application for what the apostle Paul is explaining to the Ephesian Christians about God choosing us in Christ (Ephesians 1:4).

Paul insists that God blessed each of us before we even existed, when the Lord chose to *pre-love* us. God the Father chose us *before* the foundation of the world; later he sacrificed his only Son for us even while we were *still* sinners. Determined and purposeful, God the Father pre-loves people the world over. And whether we know it or not, God pre-loved us.

I would have never appreciated the meaningfulness of this had I never experienced searching and searching for the right child to adopt and love. Perhaps by knowing some of what we went through to find our daughter, you too will begin to come to terms with the significance of being a pre-loved child of God.

A HEART'S LONGING

After being married close to five years, my wife, Sharon (or Snoopy), and I believed we had more than enough love now to add a child to our family. Our marriage was clearly not perfect, yet we felt our love for each other had been perfected enough by the Lord and life together. It felt like the right time to welcome another life into our family circle. Only the Lord knew it would take us another thirteen years before we would have this cherished desire of our hearts.

During the first three years of this period, we never shared with anyone that we were trying to start a family. Our optimism began to flag noticeably, especially as news of other pregnancies around us seemed to be popping up weekly. As the third year of futility came to an end, we agreed it was time to seek out an infertility doctor.

If you ever have to consult with a specialist in infertility, let me alert you to the blatant imbalance of the process. There's not much that needs to be said or done to the husband. The wife, however, has to endure the bulk of the probing and postulating. After preliminary tests, our doctor told us, "So far, there's no medical reason I can give you why you two shouldn't be able to conceive a child." Turning to my wife he said, "However, you might have some deeper issues that we can only explore if you consent to having some surgery." We both ignored the surgical reference and went home to keep charting our efforts dutifully on the calendar. It was still only a matter of time, right? Didn't he just say we should be able to do this?

We tried off and on for the next two years with nothing to show for our efforts but mounting disappointment and frustration. I started prodding Snoopy to have the exploratory surgery: "What if there's really something inside of you that makes it impossible for you ever to get pregnant? We could keep trying for several more years, and it won't make a bit of difference. Why not let the doctor look inside you?" I'll never forget her retort to my pleadings. "This is so unfair! You're the one that wants to be a father so much, so why can't you have the surgery? I want to have a child, but I'm not willing to let someone cut me open simply to look around. I'm sorry, but I'm not about to have surgery for someone else, not even you." Unsure what to do with my pent-up emotions, I began to question whether we even had enough love to keep us together through this ordeal, let alone more than enough to offer a child.

One night, as we pulled the car into our driveway, I revisited my mounting frustrations with Snoopy's stubborn refusal to submit to exploratory surgery. As she gave me a fresh version of her stalwart argument, something happened that completely transformed my attitude. While she was still talking, I sensed something like an invisible scalpel slicing my abdomen open from right beneath my navel down to right above my groin area. As I "looked" on with eyes of disbelief, I saw the incision widen quickly until I could see my bowels and other lower organs. In that "surgical" moment, God removed my insensitivity to my wife.

On our wedding day I had promised to love Snoopy as Christ loved the church and gave himself up for her. There in the car, God convicted me that I must die to my need to be a father because that need was causing my wife to feel like a failure. My longtime dream of being a father had to give way to my sacred vow to be the husband Jesus had called me to be. From that moment on, God began helping me lay aside all thoughts of her having surgery. What God didn't remove, though, was my heart's longing to love a child.

The Pain of Not Knowing

In an effort to turn our pain into ministry, we formed an infertility support group at church with other couples struggling to conceive. Nearly every couple at least had been given a medical reason for their difficulties. It was natural for them to make the shift to pursuing adoption and, within a couple years' time, they all became ecstatic parents. I privately envied them because they'd been given concrete reasons to move on, and we still had none. With "there's no medical reason I know why you can't get pregnant" still ringing in our ears, we finally were the only ones left.

After nearly nine years of futility, turning forty at the end of 1994 caused to me to close this chapter of our marriage. That very next spring, while enjoying a night out in Hawaii with another childless couple, I announced to them (and really to myself) that we were now officially no longer hoping to bring a child into our relationship through any means.

Only days later, Snoopy shared that her parents had sold some properties and were transferring some of their assets to their children now. "What do you suppose God wants us to do with this sudden windfall?"

I quipped, "Maybe we could remodel our house."

Snoopy carefully answered her own question. "I don't believe God wants us to invest this money in our house. God gave us this money to spend on a child. I know you've put that behind you. But I can't get around feeling that this is for us to adopt a child." And just like that, I got excited all over again.

WHERE IN THE WORLD?

Adoption. The dictionary defines this as "to take by choice into a relationship; specifically: to take voluntarily (a child of other parents) as one's own child." To us it meant choosing a child in great need to love and cherish unconditionally and without end as a member of our family. We had enough love, we had enough money, and now we had plenty of desire to do this. But where in the world should we start looking for this pre-loved child?

Right before we'd left for Hawaii, a message on our answering machine from a member of our church announced that a Korean graduate student was pregnant and wanted to place the anticipated child for adoption. The day after we got back, I phoned for more details.

We learned that the baby was going to be Korean-Nepalese and that the birth mom didn't have any insurance. For the first time we realized that the ethnicity of the child was a vital issue for us. We decided this was not the baby for us. So this first time we rejected a child that was offered to us, trusting the Lord to take good care of that baby. We had no way of knowing that for the next several years, we would be the ones rejected over and over again.

We turned to the Los Angeles County Adoption Services in an attempt to locate either a Chinese or Japanese American baby or young child. They told us that Asian American babies seldom come through their system. We attended the orientation, submitted all the paperwork and waited for a call that would never come.

Several months later, a young Chinese American woman marched resolutely up the stairs to our church offices declaring, "I need to see a priest." Already in the second trimester of an unwanted pregnancy with a Korean American young man, she'd allowed her mom to talk

her out of having an abortion early on. She was scheduled to abort
the baby the very next day, but given the advanced development of
her baby, she was terribly conflicted. I couldn't just sit there without
making a case for her going full term. "Countless Asian American
couples," I told her, "including my wife and me, are waiting for exactly the kind of baby God is growing inside of you. If you allow this
child to be born, I am positive a grateful couple will love your little
boy. I'm not asking you to let my wife and me adopt your son, but to
to give your baby a chance to have a life with a loving family."

She agreed to postpone her abortion to the following Tuesday
and take the weekend to contemplate the decision. Monday, her
mom called me. Her daughter had half-heartedly attempted sui-
cide, gone to the emergency room and was now home. She had decided to give birth to this baby, and if she decided not to keep him,
she wanted us to adopt him.

Pre-adoptive parents have their own unique forms of suffering.
Denied a nine-month gestational period, there's really nothing tangible to get excited about until the adoption is imminent. You
learn you cannot allow yourself to get excited because so many
things can happen to derail an adoption. You hunt down leads,
you get papers in order, you complete your home study, but you
don't dare do anything expectant parents would do until a real live
child is actually entrusted to you.

Sadly for us, in her eighth month this young unwed mother
told us she'd decided to keep and raise her son.

We heard about a local source for adopting babies from Japan.
From the outset, we'd determined that the child we were hoping
to adopt would be an infant girl and either Chinese (me), Japanese
(Snoopy) or some familiar Asian combination. Extending our

search across the Pacific, while expensive, held out the promise that we would actually find a suitable little baby girl to love.

So, near the end of 1995, we made the contacts and began the process of becoming qualified to adopt a child—in this case, one born outside of the United States. After a painfully long year, we were qualified, but there were still no babies in the pipeline, so we expanded our parameters to include Asian American babies from Hawaii.

While we waited, we saw many couples adopt precious children from China and Korea. Were we being too particular? Was sticking to our guns of only looking in Japan or of trying to find an Asian American baby sending us down the road to a childless future? As much as we genuinely rejoiced with our friends over their adoptions, their success made us wonder if we'd set ourselves up for constant failure.

Our mounting doubts disappeared in December 1997 when the Japanese social worker called to say that a woman was four months pregnant, and we were next in line to adopt the baby! It was a boy, but that hardly mattered to us at that point. We contacted the attorney and called off the search in Hawaii because we thought we'd finally found our child.

It was virtually impossible for us not to get excited now. For the very first time, we selected a name for our soon-to-be son, and church friends began planning baby showers for us. And yet my wife still held back the deepest part of her heart in case this too would not happen.

The little boy was born on April 24, 1998. Then a couple of photos arrived, taken of him when he was four weeks old, wrapped in a baby blue blanket. Those two pictures of Baby convinced my wife that she could finally get excited about becoming a mom. We bought a crib and, for the first time, dared to venture into baby stores to shop for linens and infant items. We felt like we were walking on clouds of joy even though we were only carrying two three-by-five pictures, not a baby.

Told that our son would come to us when he was at least three months old, we began to look forward to becoming parents in late July. But in June our excitement was turned to ashes. The adoption was off because there were indications that the baby had a serious health problem. There was nothing we could do to help him or adopt him.

This time we were utterly and completely shattered. After three years of trying to find the right child to adopt, after expending all kinds of emotions and spending thousands of dollars, we not only had nothing to show for it, but no way of proceeding. We'd been dropped to the bottom of the waiting list in Japan. We were stymied, clueless and heartbroken.

That August we were told that three healthy two-year-old boys in China needed to be adopted in two months. They were looking for three couples that had already been cleared for international adoptions. Was this something God wanted us to pursue? Though we'd always wanted a baby girl and we'd never wanted to go to China, we applied for one of these little boys.

With less than two months to get everything done and certified, we raced through the bureaucratic gauntlet at breakneck speed and met the deadline. But only days after reporting that we were good to go, the agency told us that the Chinese adoptions bureau had decided it was not going to allow three healthy boys to leave the country. Once again our adoption was off.

We weren't devastated like before because we'd vowed not to get excited. So it was pretty easy to agree when our caseworker recommended that she redirect our paperwork to adopt a two-year-old girl. All of our previous misgivings about looking in China were buried by our overwhelming desire to find the child God wanted us to love.

Our agency's director called the last week of March to let us know that she'd be in Beijing, China, to conduct business with the adoptions bureau. "I'll be meeting them at 9 a.m. on Thursday morning, April 8th. I'm hoping to bring back a picture of your child."

SURPRISE!

I purposed to pray at the exact time she was going to be meeting with these officials. So on Wednesday, April 7, at six o'clock in the evening, I sat quietly in my study and asked the Lord to speak to me, to let me know somehow if this truly was going to be the child God wanted us to love. I sat there in silence for over twenty minutes, straining with the ears of my spirit to hear God's still, small voice. I got absolutely nothing. Not a phrase or a word, not even a mild tingle. So I prayed, "Lord, I'm going to interpret your silence as telling us to keep trusting you. If that's what you want, I'm okay with that. In Jesus' name, Amen."

Twenty minutes later the phone rang. It was a couple from another church. "Hi, Ken! Want a baby? One was just born four days ago in Orange County. It's a little girl, both parents are Chinese Americans, and the birth mom is flying home in seventy-two hours. She's a nineteen-year-old Christian college student. She hasn't been able to find a couple that meets her criteria: Chinese, Christian and willing to have an open adoption. We thought of you and your wife."

What I really wanted to say was, "Yes! Yes! We've been suffering and searching all over for this exact child! Of course we want to adopt her!" However, with us merely months away from going to China and with thousands of dollars already invested in this endeavor, I felt I couldn't agree to this. Especially since my wife still hadn't come home.

I finally answered. "As we speak there is someone in Beijing right now talking to a bureaucrat about the two-year-old we're close to adopting from China. I'm tempted to jump at this opportunity, but I think we're going to have to stay the course. Let me call some couples in our church."

For the next half hour I made calls to couples I thought might be interested, interrupting their suppers, trying to talk them into adopting this baby. All this time I kept wishing we were free to pursue her. Snoopy finally came home. I exclaimed, "You wouldn't believe what happened about an hour ago. Someone called to say that there was this little Chinese American infant girl available to adopt, but you'd have been so proud of me. I wasn't impulsive. Since you weren't home, I told her that we were committed to going to China. So I've been calling around trying to find a good home for this little girl."

She was flabbergasted. "What! Are you nuts? This sounds *exactly* like the child we've been searching for all these years. Let's get that birth mother on the phone!"

I was taken aback. "What about China? What about all the money we've already spent? We're merely months away from flying over there to get her."

It was as if we'd temporarily switched personalities. She quickly replied, "We'll worry about China later. Right now, we've got to call that person back and find out how to get in touch with that birth mother." As we waited for her to call, we prayed together and the Lord seemed to be saying that, finally, this was the child he wanted us to adopt.

Those next ninety minutes seemed to take forever. Finally, at 10:30 p.m., the phone rang, and a young, unfamiliar female voice was on the other end. The birth mother! I spoke with her for over an hour. Even though we were able to establish a warm rapport rather quickly, as our conversation was naturally winding down, she never said she wanted us to adopt her daughter. I tried to give her an opening. "Since you're leaving the state in forty-eight hours, I guess you'll have to make up your mind pretty soon about what you want to do with your daughter."

Her response floored me. "Oh, I don't have any decision to make. I'm going to keep my daughter and take her back home with me."

I was tempted to lash out in anger. Instead I wished her the best, told her that if she changed her mind we'd count it a privilege to raise her daughter, and prayed for her. We knew that if she were going to change her mind, it would probably be the next night.

After an excruciatingly long day, as I walked through the front door, Snoopy had the phone to her ear as she looked up excitedly at me. She mouthed these unforgettable words: "The baby is ours!" Were we finally going to become parents tomorrow?

The next day, we had to meet for the first time, convince our respective agencies to facilitate this unusual and urgent adoption, and secure legal documents that would allow us to take the baby to the doctor even though we wouldn't be her legal parents for another six months. But the Lord removed all the obstacles, and so it was at five o'clock that afternoon in our home that the birth mom said her personal and private goodbyes to her daughter. She then placed little Janessa—only six days old—in Snoopy's waiting arms. I walked the birth mom and her entourage to the host family's van. Afraid to breathe, I waved farewell until they were out of sight. Then I raced back inside.

Snoopy looked like she hadn't moved a muscle since I'd been gone. Cradling this precious gift from God in her arms, she looked up at me with tears of joy streaming down her face and asked, "What are we going to do now? We don't even have the crib set up, and we don't have any baby supplies in the house!"

The indescribable joy of being Janessa's parents didn't erase all those times of heartache and heartbreak, didn't replace all the money we'd spent or the years we'd invested looking down blind alleys, but it did give them meaning. Now it felt like all our efforts were the ways we had pre-loved this tiny baby.

5

FULL AND FOREVER
FAMILY MEMBERS

*H*aving read our story of finding the right child to love and treasure, you're hopefully able to appreciate this fresh take on what it means for God to have *chosen* us before the creation of the world to be adopted as his sons and daughters through Jesus Christ. The apostle Paul had some specific reasons for describing the Lord's choice of us as *adoption*.

ANCIENT ATTITUDES ABOUT ADOPTION

Paul stated in Ephesians 1:5-6 that God "destined us for adoption as his children through Jesus Christ, according to the good pleasure of his will, to the praise of his glorious grace that he freely bestowed on us in the Beloved." Paul was a lawyer. He was familiar not only with Jewish law but most likely with Roman and Greek laws too since he was part of that whole Jewish Diaspora in Asia

Minor (which included ancient Greece), which was then under Roman rule. So as Paul here was using the concept of adoption in a spiritual sense, one has to wonder which adoption law he had in mind when using this metaphor? Was it the Roman version, the Jewish version or the Greek one?

During my research I discovered that it wasn't until late in the twentieth century that Jewish people actually had a legal way to adopt a child. For Jewish people, the "seed," or blood connection, is vitally important. You may remember that in the Old Testament if there could be no male heir through the wife of the husband, then it was appropriate for him to sleep with a servant girl. Jewish thinking was that the resulting child would still be part of the husband's family lineage. The concept of adopting someone who was not from the seed of your family was a very unusual and foreign concept to someone from that particular mindset.

At least the ancient Greeks were open to adopting children, although their concept of adoption at the time of Paul's writing this letter was a very limited one. It didn't have any guaranteed long-term benefits to the adoptee. If you were adopted into a Greek family back then, your father could cancel the adoption up until your eighteenth birthday. Imagine how insecure it must have felt to grow up as an adopted child in a Greek family. There was no guarantee that you would be a family member in the future; thus, there was no promise that you'd receive an inheritance someday. If your adoptive parents ever had any regrets about choosing you to love, you were history.

And then we come to the Roman version. Roman adoption law was actually rooted in the Romans' high value of family. For ancient Romans, their family values took the form of a cult of family worship. This sounds very similar to Buddhist and Confucian practices where keeping alive the memory of your patriarch's ancestors is extremely important. If a couple has no children, the whole family worship is destroyed. Throughout the movie *Gladiator* we can see in the character Maximus (played by Russell Crowe) a great example of this ancient Roman practice. After this legendary Roman general had been forced into being a gladiator, each night he would take out a little leather pouch and tenderly remove the little clay figurines of his slain wife and child and put them down on a makeshift altar. Maximus would then pray to their spirits for peace and help. Most of his seething anguish and anger was fueled more by the brutal murder of his family than by the treacherous murder of his beloved Caesar. For Rome could always find another Caesar, but where could he go to find another family?

Because of the cultlike importance of families, the Romans developed very explicit and comprehensive rules to assist childless families with adopting. First off, only the patriarch of the clan could initiate adoption. No orphan could approach a Roman father and say, "*Bon journo*, I'm an orphan, and I'd like to join your family." This had to be something that the prospective father desired and then pursued. If that was the case, then the adopting father assumed and paid for the adoptee's prior debts, because the person being adopted wasn't necessarily a baby. And so the father would normally say, "I take you; I take on all your debts, and I will pay for them. They're canceled." This assumption of all outstanding debts by the father was one of the most distinctive feature of Roman adoption.

Unlike the Jews, the Romans were not obsessed with a child being a blood descendant, so they were much more eager to adopt children than the Jews were. And in stark contrast to the Greeks, the Romans never treated adoption as a temporary attachment. According to ancient Roman law and culture, an adopted child was fully embraced by the family and was guaranteed a complete share of the inheritance, never to be cut off or rejected. In light of these factors, it sounds like Paul was referencing the Roman view of adoption when he wrote, "He destined us for adoption as his children through Jesus Christ, according to the good pleasure of his will" (Ephesians 1:5). It was clear to Paul that none of us initiated our adoption; it was our heavenly Father. And why did God the Father do this? The apostle from Tarsus reasoned that God did this simply because he had more than enough love to share: "to the praise of his glorious grace that he freely bestowed on us in the Beloved" (Ephesians 1:6). So once again we are reminded that it is only through God's pre-loving us that we can hope to become members of his family.

In citing God the Father's willingness to sacrifice Jesus, Paul appears to be comparing the aspect of Roman adoption law that guaranteed that all debts of the adoptee would be assumed and paid for in full by the adoptive father. "In him [Jesus] we have redemption through his blood, the forgiveness of our trespasses, according to the riches of his grace that he lavished on us" (Ephesians 1:7-8). Because his Son was holy, sinless and humble, our heavenly Father has everything necessary to pay for the debts of his adopted children, no matter how enormous those debts might be. God does this not because we deserve this remarkable grace, but because we are worth it to him. Isn't that astounding? Can you imagine being a forty-three-year-old orphan, with an accrual of more than four decades of debts, only to be adopted by a loving father who immediately takes care of the balances on your auto loan, mortgage, credit cards and even your gambling debts? But wait, it gets even better.

SAFE AND SECURE

From then on, with our sin-debts paid for in full, we can rest assured that we will never be cast out of the family of God. Secure in our place in God's family, we are free to delve into the mystery behind God's pursuit of us. In other words, we are confident enough to learn the story of our spiritual adoption: "With all wisdom and insight he has made known to us the mystery of his will, according to his good pleasure that he set forth in Christ, as a plan for the fullness of time, to gather up all things in him, things in heaven and things on earth" (Ephesians 1:8-10).

For real adoptees, it is a rare and amazing gift to unravel the mysteries surrounding their adoptions. We received Janessa in April 1999, but it wasn't until December that it was appropriate to appear with her in Children's Court. Surrounded by some of our closest friends from church, my wife and I proudly raised our right hands and pledged to the judge that we wanted to be her legal parents. It was such a thrill to hear him say, "And now, from this point forward, your name will be Janessa Akemi Fong, and you will be issued a new birth certificate indicating such. Congratulations!" This little girl, who had been conceived out of wedlock and whose birth parents had been quite traumatized by this unplanned pregnancy, now carried our family name and had a brand new future ahead of her.

One of the things another social worker taught us was that, even though we received Janessa when she was only six days old, we would still have to anticipate being what was called "family plus": all the issues of a typical family plus extra issues unique to being a family with an adopted child. As we started to make peace with this additional reality for our newly formed family, we already could anticipate the one colossal issue that nearly every adopted child has at some point in her life: wanting or needing to know the story surrounding her adoption. An adopted child can feel incredibly and wonderfully part of her family yet still be haunted by the mystery surrounding her adoption into it.

Legally, until quite recently, it was virtually impossible to track down information about one's birth parents because the records were typically sealed and most adoptions were considered closed. The trail is often even colder if the adopted child came from an orphanage overseas and was the result of being abandoned. I believe that with the growing popularity of open adoptions like ours, increasing numbers of adopted children will not have to live with a significant emptiness inside. A great deal, however, still depends on the willingness of the adoptive parents to dispel this mystery by telling and retelling the story of the adoption to their child in a natural and kind fashion.

The director of our birth mom's agency gave us a piece of advice before we left her office: to create a "life book" for Janessa, replete with pictures of her birth parents at various ages, to capture her unique story of becoming our daughter. She said, "Children are naturally narcissistic. They love looking at pictures of themselves. So if you put together a book about her story and read it occasionally at bedtime with her, she'll begin to learn the circumstances of her adoption in a very normal way."

After my daughter's second birthday, I began to work in earnest on assembling this, using a simple desktop publishing program on our computer. With clip art, I created collages to go along with the simple words describing our adoption quest from beginning to end. I scanned in pictures of both birth parents as well as those of many of our wonderful family and friends who came by that first week to see this little miracle firsthand. I even included pictures of us making a subsequent visit to the adoption agency and some from our special day in Children's Court. I think, though, that the most significant pictures are those of Janessa's birth mom on the day we all first met and received our daughter.

I had forgotten to include these pictures in my first version of her life book. Or perhaps I subconsciously wasn't really comfortable with our daughter making that close a connection to her birth mother. But that meant that the pictures of the birth mother in the book never showed her holding Janessa. It went from an assortment of pictures of the birth mom growing up, through her high school graduation pictures, to ones of Janessa in our arms, surrounded by all our family and friends, with no photos of the actual transition day.

Once I realized this glaring omission, I made sure to include several pictures of that very stressful but still amazing day, along with a telling of that portion of her story. They may not mean a whole lot to Janessa now, but I am sure that in the years to come, seeing herself cradled in her birth mother's arms will reinforce their special, lifelong relationship.

Our daughter, now three-and-a-half years old, knows that she has a birth dad even though thus far he has chosen not to know her. She even knows his face because of his high school pictures in her life book. There are already parts of her face that she is beginning to recognize come from his. For instance, she definitely has his smile. More significantly, she has begun to carve out a budding relationship with her birth mom, who came for her first visit when Janessa was only eleven months old and for her second during Janessa's third summer with us. My wife and I could sense that this second visit was the beginning of something very important for Janessa, for a three-year-old is already starting to memorize names and faces and, most of all, significant relationships.

The day we all spent together for her second visit only underscored this prediction, for no sooner did we all exit the car than Janessa asked her birth mom to carry her. Normally, even since then, she only asks us, her parents, to carry her. But somehow, maybe as a result of our recounting for her the story of her beginnings, this little girl sensed a special connection to this attractive young woman. For an entire summer's day, they giggled and ate and played, finishing with the birth mom giving her a bubble bath and reading her three bedtime stories. Even with the many photos and the video of this special reunion, we are looking forward to even more significant ones between them in the future.

The void in our daughter's identity is slowly being filled with the most significant person in her past—the person who carried her within her womb and nourished and protected her for nine months, the person who named her, the young lady who entrusted her to us. Instead of feeling threatened by this emerging special bond between our daughter and the woman who gave birth to her, my wife and I are thankful to God that this essential chapter in her life will not be a mystery to Janessa. To us, this will only help Janessa feel the strength of the bond between her and us.

And so, "with all wisdom and insight," our heavenly Father has explained to us in the Bible the exact circumstances surrounding our spiritual orphan status and ultimately our adoption by him in Christ Jesus (Ephesians 1:8). In Isaiah 53:6 there is a metaphorical description of how we humans became spiritually destitute and separated from God: "All we like sheep have gone astray; we have all turned to our own way, and the Lord has laid on him the iniquity of us all." Isaiah the prophet referred to us as lost sheep, a familiar comparison for most of us who are Christians.

God has peppered the Scriptures with other metaphors to describe our plight, some of which include saying that we're like adulterous women or like orphans—living as if we have no father, living as if we have no family, as if we have no one to thank but ourselves. This is a direct outcome of being sinners. Sin is what makes us forget that we've ever been kissed and is what has severed our relationship with the Father. One typical outcome of all this is that we betray God's trust and begin to worship other things as if they're gods or fathers. We might grow up not knowing anything about God's mission to seek and adopt the orphaned and lost. We have no idea that we might live for the praise of God's glory in pursuit of this mission.

In fact, we make up our own missions—missions of comfort and happiness or security and success—and we live as if we belong to no one, with no identity and no hope. We end up living without any partnership in God's mission to keep pursuing all these orphans, to try and save as many as possible. But thankfully, God is undeterred. In spite of our cluelessness and rebellion, the Father keeps pursuing us "according to his good pleasure that he set forth in Christ, as a plan for the fullness of time, to gather up all things in him, things in heaven and things on earth. In Christ we have also obtained an inheritance, having been destined according to the purpose of him who accomplishes all things according to his counsel and will, so that we, who were the first to set our hope on Christ, might live for the praise of his glory" (Ephesians 1:9-12).

The apostle Paul claims that the Father is not dissuaded by our sin and brokenness but instead is moved to come after us by our plight. Like the relentless cyborg Arnold Schwarzenegger popularized in the *Terminator* film series, the Lord keeps coming, keeps pursuing us, except that God is motivated by his abundant pre-love for us. Our heavenly Father hatched a plan—centered on Christ—to see as many children as possible brought back into his family.

The next two verses also reveal that the Lord freely gives us his Holy Spirit to reassure us further that we will forever be a part of his family. "In him [Christ] you also, when you had heard the word of truth, the gospel of your salvation, and had believed in him, were marked with the seal of the promised Holy Spirit; this is the pledge of our inheritance toward redemption as God's own people, to the praise of his glory" (Ephesians 1:13-14). We will unpack the inaugural giving of the Holy Spirit when we take a closer look at the second great kiss in Christian theology, what many of us know as Pentecost, but for now, suffice it to say that this Holy Spirit is the evidence even in us today that we will belong forever to God's special family. Paul tried to free his readers from worrying that something might one day jeopardize their family status.

A boy we know was adopted from Asia when he was three years old. He came over to our house one day with his family, and he was really fascinated with Janessa because his parents had shared with him that she, too, was adopted. Although he was your typical seven-year-old boy who'd rather be climbing trees or throwing dirt clods, that day he mainly followed Janessa everywhere, happy just to be with her no matter what unexciting toddlerthing she was into.

On another occasion, right before we were all going to sit down to dinner, I was washing her little hands at the sink. He came and stood in the doorway of the bathroom and then, very innocently and somewhat hesitantly, asked me the most interesting question. "Does Janessa live here?" He'd been to our house a number of times before, he'd seen her room, and he knew she was our daughter. So why would he ask me that question? Maybe it was because he was adopted later in life. Perhaps he has vague memories of being in an orphanage, and even at seven years old, as much as his parents and his older sibling love him unconditionally, he still has worrisome moments when he wonders how much he really is a permanent member of his family. I looked at him with as much empathy as I could muster and gently answered, "Of course she lives here. We chose her to be our daughter, just like your parents chose you to be their son. Everyone in our family lives here."

Do you ever require that kind of assurance? From time to time, many of us may need to hear the Holy Spirit whisper in our ears, "You live here. You're one of God's chosen children, and that's a forever thing. Don't doubt that; don't question that; don't worry about that. You will always be a member of God's family."

HEARTFELT HUMILITY

To be humble is an essential character trait of Christians. Paul instructed his charges to "Do nothing out of selfish ambition or vain conceit, but in humility consider others better than yourselves" (Philippians 2:3 NIV). Humble Christians have a tendency to be brutally honest with themselves; that's what keeps them from having inflated spiritual egos. While others may be quite impressed with their commitment and devotion to Christ Jesus, these believers carry around inside themselves a nagging sense of their checkered pasts or their oft-conflicted hearts and minds.

Even though the apostle Paul himself had plenty of reasons to feel superior and secure, he always knew that, given who God knew him to be and compared to Jesus' holy example, he was still by far the "worst of sinners" (1 Timothy 1:16). His heartfelt humility kept him close to his flawed humanity. Yet we never get a sense that Paul ever worried that his heavenly Father regretted choosing to love him. His tranquility must have stemmed from his innate understanding of God's pre-love for him, the self-same abundant and determined kind that moved the Lord to search for and adopt him as one of God's precious sons.

How do you handle the two-edged sword of Christlike humility? Some of us have no problem realizing how flawed and fractured God knows us to be, but knowing what a real mess we are produces private moments where we squirm nervously in the pure light of God's awareness. So although we might not have any trouble staying away from having super-inflated spiritual egos, we struggle at times to feel completely secure and at home in our relationship with God the Father.

Before learning the lessons about God's pre-love through the arduous process of becoming an adoptive dad, I secretly struggled at times for years and years to believe that my Father in heaven could know all of my flaws and foibles, yet not regret choosing me to love as a son. Even though I was baptized as a ninth grader, I remember going forward to recommit my heart to Jesus at various crusades in subsequent years. Every time I'd hear the evangelist call out to sinners to come forward to be forgiven, I'd focus on my sinful heart and mind and feel like I needed to ask for forgiveness once more, to be on the safe side.

Although I stopped doing that by the time I was around fifteen (coincidentally, I also stopped going to crusades around this age), I'd still be stricken with pangs of guilt and concern, especially when I was deliberately choosing to make sinful choices. Don't get me wrong; feeling guilt is an appropriate response to disobedience. What's not good is feeling so bad that you begin to doubt the strength of God's commitment to love you no matter what you do. Pastor and author Mike Yaconelli spoke deeply to this dilemma when he wrote: "Jesus is not repelled by us, no matter how messy we are, regardless of how incomplete we are. When we recognize that Jesus is not discouraged by our humanity, is not turned off by our messiness, and simply doggedly pursues us in the face of it all, what else can we do but give in to his outrageous, indiscriminate love?"[1]

Once I really began to grasp the unlimited scope of God's love for me, it gave me an entirely different motivation to repent of my sins. As long as I was always a bit unsure about my secure place in God's family of believers, my repentance was more fear-based than gratitude-based. In other words, I'd better repent of my sins or else my Father someday might get so fed up with me that he'd cancel the adoption and kick me out of the family of Christ. Or I'd better make sure that I obey every last one of God's commandments or else my Father is going to cut me off from my eternal inheritance. Far too many Christians live this way, exhibiting a kind of neurotic attitude toward repentance and obedience—one that grows out of being disowned by God—that makes them come across as rigid, insecure and inhumane.

On the other hand, seeing my relationship with Christ through the lens of an adoptive father helped me appreciate the permanency of my place in my Father's family of believers. Remember that forlorn Chinese toddler who was plucked from a life of certain poverty and hardship and made a family member and heir of that extremely wealthy family? As she grows up and learns that she's adopted, if she's not convinced that her parents' love for her is forever, she might entertain occasional fears that they're going to send her back someday. But if she is convinced that she is a pre-loved child and that no one and nothing will ever break her ties to the family, then her heart may overflow with indescribable gratitude. In his letter to the Galatian church, Paul again states what God the Father hopes we will all come to appreciate about what he's made possible through Christ Jesus: "But when the fullness of time had come, God sent his Son, born of a woman, born under the law, in order to redeem those who were under the law, so that we might receive adoption as children. And because you are children, God has sent the Spirit of his Son into our hearts, crying, 'Abba! Father!' So you are no longer a slave but a child, and if a child then also an heir, through God" (Galatians 4:4-7).

In real life, to be chosen for adoption may or may not place the child in a wonderful, loving family. However, to be chosen by God the Father for adoption places each of us spiritual orphans into the forever family of Christ Jesus. As in every adoption, being chosen is a pure experience of grace for the child, one that he will grow up to appreciate more and more. So even when the adopted child of God messes up or even rebels, he is moved by this grace to repent and to reconcile, safe in the knowledge that his place in the family was never in jeopardy. Repentance that comes as a response to grace is one of the clearest benefits of comprehending a relationship with God through the lens of adoption.

Paul's thoughts in Ephesians 1:17-18 capture perfectly God's desire that we reach this level of spiritual understanding about the hope, the inheritance and the amazing power that comes with being adopted into God's forever family: "I pray that the God of our Lord Jesus Christ, the Father of glory, may give you a spirit of wisdom and revelation as you come to know him, so that, with the eyes of your heart enlightened, you may know what is the hope to which he has called you, what are the riches of his glorious inheritance among the saints, and what is the immeasurable greatness of his power for us who believe, according to the working of his great power."

Here's my paraphrase of what Paul was saying to the believers in Asia Minor back then: "I'm praying for all of you. I'm praying that you are inspired by the amazing truth that God the Father has pre-loved you long before you existed and that you come to experience that Father's love more and more and more. And as you do, that you'll then come to know your Father's heart—through a spirit of wisdom and revelation—and your insecurities and fears will disappear in the light of God's love. And over time, that love that surpasses mere knowledge is bound to transform you, enabling you to access with confidence the same power that God the Father used to resurrect his Son Jesus Christ from the grave. And with that same power, God is going to enable each one of us to pre-love other people: our friends, neighbors and even enemies."

If you ever feel that the Lord has called you to serve as a missionary in the inner cities of America or in a difficult location far from where you're comfortable or welcome, one of the first things you're going to have to do is to let God teach you how to pre-love people and cultures that you don't even know or may not even like.

6

DRUNK WITH KISSES

I've never been drunk in my life, which comes as a surprise to many folks since they seem to assume that everyone's been a little tipsy at least once or twice. Then they figure that since I'm a Baptist minister, I abstain from alcohol because of my strong religious convictions. Many Christians, including a good number of Baptists, trace their abstinence to such things, but my reason is much simpler: alcohol is definitely an acquired taste, and I've never enjoyed it enough to work at it.

As a kid, I used to envy my dad tossing back a cold beer after we had both worked in the yard under Sacramento's summer sun. Reinforced in those days by the constant TV commercials for beer, his beverage looked so much more refreshing than my soft drink. Noticing my fascination, my dad finally invited me to take a sip of his beer. Boy, was my mouth surprised! Thinking it would taste like super-delicious apple juice (which it looked like), I was startled when the beer's bitter taste first accosted my taste buds. I spit it out and, ever since then, if I have an odd occasion to sip anything alcoholic, it always turns out to be the same unpleasant experience. So my not drinking those types of beverages is not a result of any strong moral convictions nor is my never having been drunk a testament to any incredible self-discipline. It's easy to resist something you don't enjoy in the least bit, and it's impossible to get drunk when you can barely down a sip. So if you've ever been drunk—though I don't encourage it—you start off knowing better than I what those first believers were experiencing in that jam-packed house when God the Father first sent his Spirit to them.

A LOSS OF INHIBITIONS

Luke's record of that first outpouring of God's Spirit onto a great number of Jesus' followers is chronicled in Acts 2:1-4: "When the day of Pentecost had come, they were all together in one place. And suddenly from heaven there came a sound like the rush of a violent wind, and it filled the entire house where they were sitting. Divided tongues, as of fire, appeared among them, and a tongue rested on each of them. All of them were filled with the Holy Spirit and began to speak in other languages, as the Spirit gave them the ability." If you are familiar with how the spiritual gift of speaking in tongues is understood and practiced today—a heavenly language unlike any language spoken on earth—you might find it thought-provoking that this very first appearance of the gift enabled the different people assembled there to communicate with one another by speaking one another's languages without any prior knowledge of them. It was as if God had put headphones on each of them, attached to some kind of universal translator gizmo à la TV's *Star Trek* series.

What I find much more intriguing is the different reactions of two sets of people who were present. Luke tells us that those who experienced this miracle of international goodwill and communication had mixed feelings of being both dumbfounded and puzzled (Acts 2:12). And who could blame them? Others present observed this cacophony of languages and cynically concluded that everyone else there must be inebriated: "They are filled with new wine" (Acts 2:13). In other words, "What's the big deal? They're all just drunk."

Peter, one of the original twelve to follow Jesus three years before, was quick to counter what was probably meant more as a dismissal than an accusation. He himself had experienced this gift of communicating in languages previously unknown to him, and he rightly understood that a dismissal was much more harmful to their reawakening movement of faith in Jesus than an accusation. A dismissal doesn't take the situation seriously enough even to charge the people with doing something wrong or seditious. As impulsive and outspoken as always, Peter was not about to take this dismissal lying down. He shouted at them, "Drunk? How can you say that about us? It's still an hour away from when we normally break our Sabbath's fast, so none of us have had breakfast, let alone any wine to drink. We are not drunk with new wine, as you say. We've just had too much of God's Spirit" (adapted from Acts 2:14-18).

Giving Peter's cynics the benefit of the doubt, why would they think this bunch of disciples of Jesus had had too much to drink that early in the day? What could there be about the behavior of Spirit-filled people that would resemble those who've imbibed too many spirits?

Certainly people who've had too much to drink lose many of their inhibitions. With some alcohol flowing through their blood streams, many people become more sociable than normal. I suppose that's why there are those who claim that they can't relax at a party until they've downed a drink or two. Some are apt to take risks they would otherwise never attempt if they were sober. Does this sound like anything that the cynics might have witnessed on that day of Pentecost?

They observed a small group of Galileans lose their natural sense of self-consciousness, enough to start conversing with all kinds of strangers in languages they might have heard before but had never uttered. Nothing can make you feel more inhibited, more uptight or more self-conscious than when you find yourself in a room full of people who are completely alien to you. And that's probably close to what the atmosphere had been like in that house in Jerusalem before God decided to do something wonderful to that band of twelve that morning, something that made them all appear as if they were drunk. But they were not drunk with wine. They were drunk with the Spirit's kisses.

THE SECOND GREAT KISS

We're back to talking about kisses. Of the two great kisses in Christian theology, the second divine kiss is the only one we might remember. The first comes when God *creates* us by filling us with his sacred breath of life, but the second takes place when Jesus, God's Son, *re-creates* us by filling us with his Holy Spirit, the most essential aspect of becoming born again. In much the same way that God the Father worked *with* Jesus to impart to each of us that first kiss of creation, the Father also works *through* Jesus to give those who desire it a second memorable kiss of re-creation, the kiss of the Spirit. Filled to overflowing with the Spirit of God, we are remade more fully alive than we possibly could be on our own.

Drunk with God's Spirit-kisses, we will eventually give evidence of losing our inhibitions and hang-ups. Maybe for the first time ever, we will find ourselves lost in the throes of worshiping the living God, without being paralyzed by the threat of being judged or criticized. Or we could be caught up in the unabashed worship of Jesus as God's Son and Lord of the universe and then—shazzam!—suddenly our hearts have been taken captive by God's heart for us and for the world.

The more uninhibited we become in our worship of God, the more eagerly we want to partner with Jesus in his mission of mercy and love to rescue spiritual orphans, wherever they are, so they too might know their Maker and revel in his kisses, joining the delirious throngs that are worshiping the Lord in spirit and truth. To the uninitiated, this kind of thinking and behavior is far from sober and sane, so the natural conclusion is that folks like these must have had way too much alcohol to drink. But to those who have come to know Jesus and have received that second divine kiss already, these alterations in outlook, mood and behavior are the results of having too much of the Spirit to drink. If this is the case, then party on!

It wasn't enough for Peter to demand that their critics not dismiss them all as being drunk and disorderly. He seized this opportunity to try to convince his audience, most of whom were Jews, that Jesus was responsible for all the wild and inexplicable behavior (Acts 2:5-11). First, Peter brought up the greatest hero of faith for all Jews, King David, reminding them that as great as

David was, he died and is still dead to this day (Acts 2:29). But David knew enough about what God was up to that he pointed beyond himself to the day when one of his direct descendants (here again, you can appreciate the Jewish emphasis on seed) would inherit his vacant throne. But as great a king as David was, the coming king would be far, far greater. He would die, yes, but he would not stay dead long. He was to be the one true Savior for the world (Acts 2:30-31).

In Psalm 132:11, David wrote of a time when God promised this would happen: "The Lord swore to David a sure oath from which he will not turn back: 'One of the sons of your body I will set on your throne.'" Peter was trying to convince these Jewish cynics that Jesus of Nazareth was this no-longer-dead descendant of David—the Messiah.

Peter really got their attention when he essentially said, "Whether or not you liked Jesus when he was here, you just can't dismiss the fact that his tomb is missing a body. You might have different theories to explain the disappearance of Jesus' corpse three days after it was sealed in there, but none of us can explain his post-resurrection appearances when he was here among us in Jerusalem for nearly a month and a half. He then returned to his Father's right side, where he was given the Holy Spirit, and as promised, Jesus poured out his Spirit on his followers. That's what you just witnessed. That's what happened in here about twenty minutes ago, all those people speaking a multitude of languages and reaching out beyond their own circle of friends, remember? You naturally assumed they had all been drinking early this morning, when actually they are delirious with delight that Jesus' Holy Spirit has 'kissed' them to a brand new life" (taken from Acts 1:3;

2:32; John 14:26; Acts 2:33). Peter implored them to move beyond their reverence for David to know without any doubt that "God has made him both Lord and Messiah, this Jesus whom you crucified" (Acts 2:36).

No sooner had Peter received that second great kiss from God than he began to witness unashamedly to a less-than-friendly crowd. It follows that if we too have received the Holy Spirit from Jesus, we will be mobilized to witness boldly and often to those who don't believe. Yet how many of us who've received this second great kiss of the Holy Spirit have freely done so? Even after being a Baptist pastor all these years, I often still feel inhibited when I contemplate sharing my faith in Christ with others. Many people today frown on Christians who try to convert people, viewing us as heavy-handed and intolerant; as a result, a good number of us have been frightened into silence. However, infused as we are with the Spirit of God, there's every reason to believe that Jesus has provided each of us with the means to overcome even our strongest inhibitions so his saving message will have the opportunity to sink in where it's needed most—people's hearts.

HITTING HOME IN THEIR HEARTS

Luke writes that a great number of those people who had initially dismissed the Spirit-kissed disciples as being drunk responded to Peter's preaching of the gospel message with an overwhelming sense of conviction. "Now when they heard this, they were cut to the heart and said to Peter and to the other apostles, 'Brothers, what should we do?'" (Acts 2:37). At that very moment, they believed themselves to be some of those pre-loved prodigals that God had been on a mission to bring back into his family, no matter how great the cost, no matter how long it took. They then wanted to know what to do with this realization.

It was like saying to Peter, "We now believe that Jesus is our Lord and long-awaited Messiah. We believe that what we have witnessed this morning is not a result of drinking wine but of drinking deeply of God's Spirit. We too now wish to be drunk with the Spirit of God. We too want to worship the Lord God freely and completely. We want to be free to do whatever the Lord Jesus wants us to do. Brothers, we eagerly desire that second divine kiss. We want what Jesus breathed into all of you that has made you less self-conscious and more God- and kingdom-conscious. What should we do next?"

Peter could hardly believe what he'd heard. These fellow Jews from near and far were now poised to become followers of Jesus! He spoke plainly and directly so that none of them might misunderstand what was required of them: "Repent, and be baptized every one of you in the name of Jesus Christ so that your sins may be forgiven; and you will receive the gift of the Holy Spirit" (Acts 2:38). To begin a new life, one characterized by freedom and the embodiment of the holy life and teachings of God's Son, you must first confess to Jesus that you are a sinner in need of his forgiveness. Each of us must recognize how foolhardy it is to be a precious child of God yet live as if we are fatherless and alone.

Perhaps confessing that Jesus is God's Son and our Savior should only happen after first acknowledging that we are God's children whom God kissed into existence and that we have lived estranged from him ever since, even though God has been our unknown benefactor. Ashamed of our ungratefulness and rebellion, we then begin to turn our lives completely around, filled to overflowing with God's love and kisses. Peter referred to this transformation as "repentance," a wholesale, 180-degree change of heart, mind and direction as a response to waking up to the astounding grace of God, who pre-loves us all. As laid out near the end of the previous chapter, I believe it's crucial that we each understand repentance as a *response* to God's grace instead of seeing repentance as a *prerequisite* for receiving God's grace. This is an extremely critical truth that merits some further study here.

Far too many of us have the order of these two fundamental doctrines reversed and, as a result, end up leading anxious, virtually graceless lives. Other graceless teachers, preachers and authors have drilled it into our heads that we must earn God's grace, striving strenuously to prove that, like the older brother of the prodigal son in Luke 15, we are worthy someday of a grace party. We endeavor to have daily devotions, never miss a worship service or prayer meeting, serve in a multitude of ministries and give away as much as we can. And all of this is done with the hope that eventually God will deem it sufficient and we will have deserved his favor at last. But we never feel like we are doing enough; there is always more that God requires. As a result, we are quick to judge and reluctantly extend grace and mercy to others and ourselves. After all, why should anyone else get a break when his efforts at repentance are far inferior to mine and I have yet to get my share of grace from God?

In stark contrast, repentance that is a response to being unconditionally pre-loved and permanently adopted in God's family overflows with gratitude and generosity, even though it, too, is focused on being obedient and faithful to the Lord. In this case, however, God's perfect love removes any fear of being punished or cast aside because we still aren't good enough Christians or because we have failed or fallen so far.

This quiet confidence is rooted in the fact that "there is no fear in love, but perfect love casts out fear; for fear has to do with punishment, and whoever fears has not reached perfection in love. We love because he first loved us" (1 John 4:18-19). God had more perfect love than he needed, so he created the heavens and the earth. He took great delight in making us humans in his image, so that we alone are God's children, and in paying the highest price to bring us back home to him (1 John 3:1). Starting a new life in Christ with the recognition that you are a precious, pre-loved child of God is the key to pursuing a lifetime of repentance with a thankful heart instead of a fretful one. True repentance is a *response* to God's grace not a *requirement* to receive it.

With this grace-before-repentance sequence in mind, Peter's commandment to be baptized now sounds more like an outward expression of gratitude to Jesus than a rigid requirement that one must fulfill immediately or else. To be baptized as a response to God's grace and love is another way to declare to others how grateful you are to be loved so extravagantly by the Lord. It is a means not only for new believers to experience a tangible expression of what Jesus has already invisibly accomplished in their hearts but also to declare their membership in the body of Christ, his church. Jesus wants to save the world one person at a time, but he wants to join together every believer on earth so they are a new people, members of his body, as expressed and experienced through local churches. One of the most significant changes that grace-based repentance brings about is the creation of a people of God who come to relate to each other as members of the same family with the same Father.

Peter also declared to his listeners that with their sins now forgiven by Christ, the way would be clear for them to receive the same Holy Spirit the disciples had received earlier. They too could become drunk with this second spectacular kiss from God, filled this time with God's breath of new life in Christ (Acts 2:38).

The promise of forgiveness and anointing was not only for those assembled in Jerusalem that day. And it wasn't only for their Jewish relatives yet to be born. This promise from the Lord was for "all who are far away, everyone whom the Lord our God calls to him" (Acts 2:39). It's for you! It's for me! It's for all your friends and neighbors! And it's for all the people living everywhere in the world! To know God as Father is to know that our Father's heart is determined to salvage and save as many spiritual orphans as possible. His promise is both timeless and global. And it involves all of us whom God has blessed with this second great kiss.

Peter's words were empowered by God's Spirit so that on the day the multitude gathered to hear him speak of God's undying, undiluted love for all his orphaned children, three thousand people declared their desire to be drunk with God's kisses too (Acts 2:40-41). By the power of the Spirit, they were reborn into a new identity with a new set of values and a whole new sense of belonging to God, loving him as a grateful response, loving the people God loves and opening their entire lives to one another (Acts 2:42-47). All of this came as a result of the second great kiss, the divine kiss of the Holy Spirit of God.

THE KISS OF THE KISS

I had been a Christian already for more than twenty years and a pastor for nearly ten when I first attended the Urbana Student Mission Convention in December 1990. I can recall being challenged by the speakers, but it was during the times of worship with nearly twenty thousand missions-minded college students that I remember feeling intoxicated. It felt as if I was receiving a fresh kiss of God's Spirit, and as much as I loved God already, I was moved to love him more—or at least express my love of God more tangibly than I had ever done before.

The first thing the Spirit began stripping away was my self-consciousness. Instead of being so focused on myself and what was important to me, I found myself becoming more aware of God's holiness and the priority of his mission to rescue lost and hurting people. The Spirit began to remove my inhibitions so that I found myself increasingly willing to pre-love people I didn't know, or knew but didn't love. As my love for God grew, so did my desire to go and be with the unconvinced and the overlooked. But where did God want me to go and whom specifically did he want me to be with?

Being inundated each day for nearly a week with the hurting or hidden people in the world, I was at first uncertain how I was going to "go" while believing God had called me to be a pastor at the church I'd served since 1981. But I received direction during the course of the convention. I never heard an actual voice, but the message from God was still quite clear: "Be my witness among a hidden people group right there with you in Los Angeles, a group that most evangelical Asian American Christians avoid at all costs—politically liberal activists in the Asian American community."

If this was a divine direction, I felt extremely threatened by it. Typically, people like that are virulently anti-Christian. They know too much about how Western Europe's missionaries had subjugated peoples in the New World. They look at Christianity as a white person's religion and believe that any Asian American who professes to be one is a sellout who is culturally clueless and impotent in helping others. I'd have to be drunk or crazy to try to make headway there.

After a couple of false starts, God's Spirit opened an unexpected door for me to teach a monthly Bible-based lesson to recovering addicts and alcoholics at the Asian-American Drug Abuse Program (AADAP) in the Crenshaw district of LA. Ever since, God has shown me how easy it is not only to love and respect alcoholics, drug addicts, former prostitutes, thieves and homeless people, but also to love and respect the many staff who guide them through this difficult program. I've earned enough trust over the years to be asked to speak at their graduation banquets, and not long ago I was invited to join their governing board. Doesn't it seem odd that a suburbanite who's never been drunk or stoned now has spent more than a decade in the 'hood, hugging society's rejects and often partnering with ideological adversaries? The best explanation I can offer is that these are the actions of a person drunk with God's kisses.

Leonard Sweet tells the story of Benjamin West, a famous American artist. As the story goes, West became a painter because of an incident with his little niece Sally. While she napped one afternoon, the young lad attempted to draw her beautiful smile. When his mother and older sister came back in the house unannounced, he panicked. West tried to hide his drawing, but his mother discovered it and looked at it closely. Far from being angry she exclaimed, "I declare he has made a likeness of little Sally." And then she kissed young Benjamin. West claimed that "ever since that day, my mother's encouraging kiss in the dark made me a painter."[1]

Sweet concludes the episode: "Our lives, like Jesus himself . . . are a kind of 'kiss of love' from heaven to earth and a 'kiss in the dark' to those who are hiding and afraid and in trouble. Jesus brought together people hiding in the dark—people who never talked together, people who never ate together, people who never drank together, even people who never touched each other—and Jesus brought them into the light, showed them one another, and showed them a way for greater sanity, a way of greater sanctity."[2]

Or as St. Bernard of Clairvaux put it, Jesus has called us to be the kiss of the kiss. Are you drunk enough now to run around kissing orphaned strangers, outcasts and enemies with Jesus' kiss of new life? There's an entire world that hasn't been kissed yet, and we have the opportunity to be God's kiss to them.

7

THE ONLY ONE WORTH
LOVING SO MUCH

*B*eing convinced of the permanence of our Father's love for us as his adopted children does wonders to alleviate our anxieties over our personal shortcomings and failures. But there are external sources of worry for us, too, when so much in the world around us is chaotic, falling apart or buried under layers of hatred or apathy. Does God offer further reassurance to enable us to keep trusting in his goodness and love in the face of so many disturbing matters around us? An age-old problem for Christians, this might best be remedied if we look again to the Scriptures to see who the divine Jesus really is and where he's taking everything. A great place to start is by being more attuned to God's special sense of time.

I'll never forget my first experience with eBay. In case you've been stranded on a desert island with no access to the Internet in the last ten years or so, eBay is an online auction house where you can find virtually anything you're looking to buy. I decided to check it out. I typed in a particular golf club and, within seconds, a list of more than a hundred of those clubs appeared on my screen. Perusing this mind-boggling array, I finally found exactly what I was looking for, close to my price range, and with only five other bidders. I typed in my maximum bid, and in mere seconds my screen name came up declaring that I was the new highest bidder. This was absurdly simple.

The eBay screen indicated that there were five days and a number of hours and minutes until the end of this online auction. Over the next three or four days I went back to check on the status of things, and each day, I was still the highest bidder. I had every reason to believe I was going to win the auction.

With only three hours to go, I was the highest bidder, and there had been no activity since my bid. I went outside and worked in the yard for a few hours to pass the time. Confident that I had won, I even ran a few errands in my car.

I returned to my computer about twenty minutes after the auction was over. To my shock and bewilderment, the screen declared that I'd lost. Lost? How could I have lost? Apparently, while I was out, eBay had sent me a message five minutes prior to the end, warning me that I'd been outbid by five dollars. I was crushed. It was clear by the screen name that the winner of this auction had never made any of the earlier bids. So who was this, and how was this person able to sneak up on me like that?

My friends who use eBay regularly told me that my experience was very typical. I was astonished to hear that there are people who lurk out there in the eBay bushes, unknown and unseen.

They watch and wait; then without warning, five minutes before the auction ends, they bid sometimes only a penny more than the highest bid, and if you're not there to react, you lose.

It didn't take me long to find another club from a different seller that matched my specifications. As before, I typed in my opening bid, but this time I couldn't care less if I was the highest bidder or not. I was content now to lurk, to blend into the background and wait for the perfect opportunity to pick off my unsuspecting competitors. With six days to wait, I went about my regular activities. I went to church and to the office. I made hospital visits, and I sat in meetings. I spent time with my family, and I even went to the driving range. Outwardly, nothing was out of the ordinary, but inwardly I was acutely aware of the tick-tick-ticking of the eBay clock as those crucial last minutes drew closer. I didn't care what time my watch said it was. Engaged in this battle of guts and stealth, eBay time was the only time that mattered.

When the day finally arrived, I spent the last three hours in front of my computer, doing other things, but always checking back to see if there was any final activity, looking for evidence of fellow cyber-lurkers. There hadn't been any for forty-eight hours, but I'd learned my lesson the hard way. As the time grew shorter, I kept hitting the refresh button more frequently, to make certain that I had the absolute latest view of the bidding. My stomach churned as the clock ticked down to one hour, then thirty minutes, then ten minutes and then five. During the final minute the clock began rolling off the seconds, and my heart started beating faster and faster as I kept refreshing my view of the bidding record. Finally, the time ran out, and the coveted club was mine! Too bad it didn't improve my golf game.

DOES ANYONE REALLY KNOW WHAT TIME IT IS?

Did you know that in Luke 24 the resurrected Jesus announced that there is a kingdom clock that is tick-tick-ticking away? Most Christians claim to believe in this alternate but ultimate scheme of time, but few make plans with this in mind. Even as those who are supposedly drunk with the Holy Spirit, we still get so caught up in everything else that's going on in our lives and in the world that we start living as if there's no other mode of time than the standard clock and calendar kind. Many of us live as if the kingdom clock were merely one of God's scare tactics, his way of motivating us to remain faithful and to convince others to follow Jesus before time supposedly runs out and God's judgment is brought to bear against all of human history.

It's tempting and easy not to take this seriously, even though Jesus said we should. The early Christians didn't have that problem. From the moment they were adopted into God's family, they lived each day acutely aware of the kingdom clock's countdown. Their awareness transformed their view of suffering and persecution, altered their ambitions and inspired them to pre-love people they had never even met. Those early Christians had what we would call *apocalyptic expectations*.

Some of the first to find faith in Jesus as Lord and Messiah expected the world to end in their lifetime; they assumed God was bringing history to the great climactic culmination spoken of in Revelation. But that was over two thousand years ago. As twenty-first-century believers, with so many concerns and distractions now shoehorned into our PDAs and daily planners, it's no real surprise that we struggle to believe there is a kingdom clock relentlessly marching us all toward Judgment Day and eternity. But a spellbinding vision God gave to a particular early Christian can help to give us a heightened sense of apocalyptic expectation in the midst of our own set of circumstances. Just as learning more about God's pre-loving us can help alleviate anxiety about the Lord's response to our personal shortcomings, learning more about how God is moving through all of human history can strengthen our faith in Jesus even if the world around us looks Godforsaken.

INQUIRING MINDS WANT TO KNOW

The book of Revelation hails from a very unique and historic literary genre. The word "revelation" itself comes from the Latin translation of the Greek word *apokalyptō*, which is where we get the word "apocalypse." Most of the time I don't think of a revelation and an apocalypse in the same sentence. Typically, an apocalypse is understood as some impending horrible cataclysm, but the word takes on a very different nuance if you think of it also as a revelation. It's not necessarily simply a prediction of gloom and doom. Apocalypse or revelation is really a picture of what is to come. This is underscored by the literal meaning of *apokalyptō*, which is "to uncover, to reveal, to disclose what is hidden."[1] Even back then, inquiring minds wanted to know what was supposed to be coming.

Apocalyptic writing was not exclusive to the author of Revelation. This type of writing was hugely popular with Jews and Christians during the three hundred-year period before and around Christ. During their two hundred-year Babylonian exile, the Jews were influenced by their Persian captors, who had a huge appetite for this genre of writing. Some Jews decided to write their own versions of these futuristic stories and, with time, learned that such apocalyptic pieces could also serve a very useful purpose:

writing such as the book of Revelation could be used as a practical call to arms against present foes in their own day.

We face oppressors in our own lives, and we desperately need to believe God has not abandoned us and is still working for our benefit. Even though it often appears that we're losing the battle, we desperately need reasons to believe his kingdom clock is yet counting down, and Yahweh God is going to win the war. God continues to utilize ancient apocalyptic literature, like the book of Revelation, to keep the flame of faith alive in us as we personally grapple with difficult times, as we are discouraged by the headlines and outraged by acts of terror. It's easy to start believing it's hopeless, to stop caring or trying to make a difference in the name of Jesus, or to fear that your adoptive heavenly Father has abandoned you in a cold and scary world. That's when we especially need to focus once more on the description of how the Lord God is going to end this story. Knowing ahead of time how this story is going to end gives us an immense advantage. No matter how nasty and nuts it gets in the middle of the story, we can be faithful through it all because we know it's going to end in the right way.

THE FINAL SCORE

In the autumn of 1974, the University of Southern California and Notre Dame University varsity football teams were resurrecting their almost annual legendary rivalry on the gridiron. Their storied competition in football has produced a great many classic memories, but this particular game in 1974 was the occasion for one of the most remarkable comebacks of any football team. In the first half, the Fighting Irish of Notre Dame were dominating the proud Trojans. At halftime, USC was down by several touchdowns. But on the ensuing second-half kickoff, USC's All-American tailback Anthony Davis caught the ball and ran it all the way back for a touchdown. This sudden turn of events was all the catalyst the Trojans needed as they roared back in those final two quarters to snatch the victory from Notre Dame's grasp. Davis scored four touchdowns in the second half to upend Notre Dame's confidence and capture the win.

I know a Trojan football fan who has that famous game on videotape. Every Thanksgiving he watches it. Because he already knows how the game is going to end, when his team is getting trounced in the first half, he keeps on laughing and hoping (doesn't this sound like drunken behavior?) because he already knows how this game is going to end.

That is the purpose of the book of Revelation. No matter how badly we're getting beaten now, regardless of how bleak it looks at halftime, God has already shown us the final score: the devil, nothing; God, everything. All of God's creation, no matter how fallen, broken or lost, is going to be found and restored if they respond to his invitation to a wonderful, intimate, lasting relationship with God the Father, God the Son and God the Holy Spirit.

Now whom do we have to thank for telling us the final score? It was a Jewish Christian who was probably in a Roman penal colony on the island of Patmos. Some people think it was the same author as the Gospel of John; other people say it can't possibly be. He tells us his name is John. His purpose was the same as a number of other writers of apocalyptic literature in that time: to embolden Christians in a Roman-dominated Asia Minor who were being persecuted for refusing to worship the maniacally egotistical emperor of the Roman Empire.

This cult of emperor worship is a critical piece of background information in studying Revelation. John was reaching out to Christians who were being harshly persecuted and killed for their adamant refusal to bow to the Roman ruler. In short, using their apocalyptically coded language, this is what he was trying to get across: "No matter how hard it gets, no matter how much they're making you suffer, no matter how great your losses are, you must keep believing that the Lord God still loves you and is still the supreme and sovereign Lord of all. In spite of how it looks now, the evildoers will be punished one day, and the righteous will be saved. Jesus has revealed to me the final chapter of human history so you might have solid reasons to keep believing in God's love for you as adopted sons or daughters, as well as reasons to keep believing in your place in God's forever family and his holy mission."

Knowing the ultimate end of the story enables us to keep believing that our holy God will have the last word and the final victory. God didn't go to all the trouble to pre-love us and adopt us after a long and costly search only to abandon us. He has demonstrated once and for all that though we're still sinners, we're always worth loving. So even in the throes of unspeakable persecution and hardship, God is still worthy of our ongoing love and trust.

WHO IS WORTHY?

John uses apocalyptic language unfamiliar to us to describe a climactic scene, starting in Revelation 5:1: "Then I saw in the right hand of the one seated on the throne a scroll written on the inside and on the back, sealed with seven seals." In verse one, John tells us what the Lord chose to reveal to him about the coming climax. God Almighty will be seated on his throne, clutching a rolled-up manuscript in his right hand. Back then messages were typically written on parchment scrolls and then rolled up and sealed with wax. Molten wax was poured onto the outside seam of the scroll, and then a distinctive stamp was pressed into the still-malleable wax to identify the sender and to ensure the integrity of the message while in transit.

In John's vision, this particular scroll was sealed with not one but seven seals, which itself would have been quite unusual. However, some Bible scholars believe that these seven seals may not have all been affixed on the exterior seam, but that each separate section of prophecy in this singular scroll had its own wax seal on the inside. If true, the reader would have had to break each seal to get to the next section. Quite honestly, I'm not sure how all that would have worked, but God gave this vision to John, not me. We do know that seven is considered a perfect number in the Bible, so this could have been symbolic of how crucial this scroll's message was. John later describes in detail the contents of this scroll, indicating that this is a narration of the coming judgment of God—what the Lord is going to do and what he is going to pronounce when he brings all of human history to a magnificent conclusion. This divine document spells out God's judgments on the wicked and his mercy to the faithful.

John next describes a mighty angel who issues a daunting challenge (Revelation 5:2-3). The angel essentially says, "God's got the scroll in his hands; who is worthy enough to unwrap this most sacred of scrolls to pronounce God's judgment on his entire creation?" This was not about finding someone who had the ability to read the words on this scroll; it was about finding someone who was qualified to speak the Lord's judgment. Interestingly enough, there aren't any takers. Nobody steps up and takes the scroll from God's hand and proclaims the message with the vision John was promised in chapter 4, verse 1. Then, according to Revelation 5:4, John begins to weep bitterly because no one is found worthy to open the scroll and read it. It's as if he is crying out, "God, what's going on here? You already know how the story ends, and you've shown me the scroll on which the final chapter is written. But there's nobody to read it!" Wouldn't you be frustrated, too?

And then the elder steps up in verse 5 and says, "Ah, but that's where you're wrong, John. There is one—and only one—who is worthy to open the scroll by breaking those seven seals. He is Messiah, the Lion of Judah, from the line of King David: Jesus. Because he conquered sin through his own death, he alone is worthy to utter God's judgment because he is the Lamb." John continues, "Then I saw between the throne and the four living creatures and among the elders a Lamb standing as if it had been slaughtered, having seven horns and seven eyes, which are the seven spirits of God sent out into all the earth" (Revelation 5:6).

Lamb is one of John's favorite terms. In Revelation he refers to Jesus close to thirty times as the "Lamb." But here in verse 6 this reference is unlike any lamb we have ever read in the balance of the New Testament. This Lamb bears the marks of slaughter, exactly as predicted in Isaiah 53:6-7. Isaiah had prophesied that the sacrificial lamb for the sins of the entire world must be slaughtered to pay the hefty price for our sins. And those marks of his slaughter are mute testimony to his worthiness to open the scrolls. But the picture that John paints for us here does not sound like a little lamb waiting to be slaughtered. Even though Jesus is that sacrificial Lamb of God, this is not the Jesus-Lamb we're used to envisioning.

FIRST BLOOD

A lamb waiting to be offered as a ritual sacrifice is small and defenseless. Certainly as the Son of God, Jesus was completely capable of halting the efforts to execute him on a cross. Yet he chose to offer no defense because this was the price of adopting the orphaned sinners in the world. And now, in John's vision of Jesus as the resurrected Lamb of God, we can appreciate Christ's determination and strength that may not have been as obvious before. It is important that we understand this picture that John is putting before us. At the risk of having you think of Jesus as the solitary, muscled mercenary popularized by Sylvester Stallone in the 1982 film *First Blood,* this description of Jesus makes me want to call him "Lambo." This is a conquering, triumphant Lamb, disfigured and bloodied because he chose to die for the sins of the world, to pay the price to adopt us all. The picture of Jesus about to pronounce judgment on us may be more symbolic than actual, but the Lord would not have included it if it weren't really important that we see Jesus in this unfamiliar and unsettling way.

Can you imagine people's reactions if we removed all the pictures of the Jesus we know so well, with his gentle expression and his outstretched, unmarred hands resting on the heads of small, smiling children? What if we took all those down from the Sunday school walls and instead hung up the portrait of the Jesus in Revelation 5:6, with his multiple menacing horns and myriad all-seeing eyes? I can almost guarantee that angry parents would have those confiscated in a flash, even though this image is taken straight off the pages of the Bible. As uncomfortable as it makes us, it's worth trying to decipher why the Spirit of God made this a part of the image of the Lamb of God that John envisioned in his dream.

Much better than us, John's audience knew all about apocalyptic writings and how to interpret them. They would have understood this to be a metaphorical depiction of the risen Christ rather than a literal one. They would have known right away that the seven horns and seven eyes were images of the Davidic Messiah. They would have known that the horn is a symbol of power in the Old Testament. And they would have easily recognized the significance of utilizing what they believed to be a perfect number: seven. The features that make us squirm would have brought them great comfort, for those seven horns mean that the Messiah has absolute power. This risen and exalted Lamb lacks nothing. There may be other powers in the universe, but there is no power that can equal the power of this Lamb of God.

And how can we forget that this fierce Lamb of God also has seven eyes? Blocking out those seven horns on his forehead for the moment, try to picture the Jesus you know with seven eyes. Too weird, right? Here again, John's Christian audience would have known immediately that, in this genre, the eye represents omniscience, the ability to know things. For Jesus to have seven, the perfect number, is to claim that this Lamb of God is not only all-powerful but also all-knowing.

Living as a pre-loved, adopted child of God can be amazing, but that doesn't mean there won't be times of confusion, chaos or consternation. So isn't it reassuring to believe that there is nothing that Jesus does not comprehend about the world, the lost, different cultures and different religions? You and I may try to figure out all these complexities, but isn't it comforting to know that the only One worthy to open the scroll of judgment is the only One capable of being the final judge because he knows absolutely everything?

There are times when we rightly celebrate Jesus' humble choice to come to our world as a human being. But we need to remind each other that Jesus is also God. Many of us focus only on the Jesus who became a human being and forget his full divine status as equal to the Father (Philippians 2:8-11). So the image John is painting here is the picture of Jesus once again and forever in all of his majesty and glory, and in all of his dimensions. That's the image God wants us to have when we envision Jesus as Judge when the kingdom clock finally stops its countdown.

A HIGHER FORM OF KISSING

It's this Jesus in Revelation 5:7-8 who reaches up to the Father and takes the scroll from his hand and prepares to open it by breaking the seals. As he does this, those around the throne begin to worship him. The four living creatures and the twenty-four elders pay him homage, worshiping the awe-inspiring Lamb of God. Worship is ascribing worth to one who is more worthy than you. In the beginning of this book we referred to worship as kissing. The behavior here is like a higher form of kissing. The worshipers' actions declare that they fully realize that Jesus alone is worthy of their worship and devotion.

Have you been a Christian for a long time yet still find worshiping Jesus to be a stiff and somewhat empty experience? Or if you are not a Christian, have you found yourself in a worship service where most of the folks around you were so caught up in worshiping Jesus that it seemed like they were drunk? Unless you have come to appreciate and experience the unfathomable love that Jesus has for you and the rest of the world, worshiping him will not be a spontaneous outpouring of love for him, nor an endless expression of your gratitude to God for choosing you to love.

Since I grew up in the church, I have always known about Jesus. And for nearly thirty years, I merely endured worship services, just going through the motions. Until I finally saw that even though I was an accomplished and good person, I was still a destitute spiritual orphan without real hope or a future until Jesus paid for my adoption into God's forever family. I think of what my life would have been like outside the circle of God's love, and I stop to appreciate anew the blessing of being one of God's children. Then the echoes of the kingdom clock counting down until Judgment Day don't strike fear in me; rather they make me long for the moment when Jesus will call me to his throne by name. Whatever I have enjoyed with him up till then will be eclipsed by the unlimited relationship with Jesus in all his infinite splendor and majesty.

8

A New Song for a New Family

*A*s you learn to celebrate being adopted into our Father's forever family in Christ, are you also celebrating the incredible diversity of that special faith community? Far too many of us stop short of this because, in many cases, we're still feeling anxious about our own place in this family as children that God the Father adopted. How can we fully embrace the many different members of our extended faith family when we're still struggling to feel secure ourselves? Without the security that springs from the perfect and abundant love of God, it comes as no surprise that we are content to live out our faith with those apparently most like ourselves—culturally, theologically, politically and so on—even though we anticipate that heaven will be incredibly diverse. But if that's how we end up living out our faith on earth, then one has to wonder how we're going to handle the mind-boggling diversity of heaven. Or

didn't you know that you've been adopted into a family that's un-
imaginably diverse?

The Lord God gave John a preview of this ultimate pending
family portrait, not only of its background but also its vocational
identity. He wrote, "They sing a new song:

'You are worthy to take the scroll
    and to open the seals,
for you were slaughtered and by your blood you ransomed
        for God
    saints from every tribe and language and people and nation;
you have made them to be a kingdom and priests serving our
        God,
    and they will reign on earth.'" (Revelation 5:9-10)

Only Jesus is worthy to open and read the divine judgment
scroll. The Bible claims that he has accomplished two things
through his sacrifice. First, by paying the price for the world's sins
with his own life, Jesus has enabled God the Father to adopt children of every description and from every possible place, forming
them into a new *family* unlike any other. Second, Jesus has established for each of God's adopted children a new *identity* as priests
of God, serving him and his kingdom purposes anywhere the Lord
directs them to go on earth.

DIVERSITY IN THE PRESENT FAMILY

Our heavenly Father didn't go to all the trouble of adopting us
only to see us avoid many of our brothers and sisters in Christ.
Nor does he allow us to claim to be Christ's heaven-bound followers without changing our understanding of our role as servant-

ministers of the good news. In other words, though some of us may have been Christians most of our lives, we may have rarely explored or pursued racial reconciliation. Additionally, being a Christian is as much about receiving a new vocation as it is about receiving a new life; your heavenly Father adopted you not only to join his family but to join in the family "business"—announcing and embodying the hope that emanates from the cross of Jesus.

It took me over twenty years to believe that being adopted by God meant I was a priest of his kingdom, and it wasn't until 1996 that I began to more fully embrace my membership in Jesus' diverse new family.

I grew up in a pretty typical Chinese American family. Becoming a baptized Christian and church member in ninth grade only seemed to underscore the fundamental values that were ingrained in our Chinese American cultural paradigm. Obey your parents. Stay out of trouble. Study hard. Work earnestly, and don't waste money. Most of all, apply all of these virtues so that you grow up to do something that your parents can brag about to their friends. It almost seemed like becoming a Christian was merely another clever way for Chinese American parents to reinforce their Confucian-based values in their children.

I'm sure that what I've described is duplicated across many cultures, but I can only speak from my own context. Oh sure, somewhere along the way I was taught that I now belonged to a new diverse family in Christ that superseded my biological one, but in those days, the non-Chinese family members might as well have lived on the moon! Everywhere I looked, all I would see were other Chinese American faces in my new extended Christian family. And it definitely looked like this was the same scenario for every other clique of Christians, not just the Chinese American ones. So though we were all taught that heaven was going to be filled with "saints from every tribe and language and people and nation," apparently few of us believed that our common future should affect or influence the ethnic and cultural ingredients of our Christian communities now. The fact that eleven o'clock on Sunday morning is still the most segregated hour in America is of little or no concern to the vast majority of Christians, even now. Does it really bother you? It certainly didn't perturb me one bit for nearly my entire life as a Christian. Diversity could wait until heaven.

FAMILY JOB: PRIESTHOOD?

Like most Chinese American kids back in the sixties and seventies, since I seemed halfway intelligent, I was regularly encouraged to grow up to be a medical doctor, which was treated as the highest possible profession. In retrospect, I can understand much better how, back when there were definite glass ceilings over most Chinese Americans' heads, becoming a medical doctor was one of the few known ways of circumventing portions of that racist structure. All people like me had to do was study harder than most of the other kids, get involved in a good number of extracurricular activities while in high school, graduate from a prestigious university with honors and pass my entrance exams with flying colors, and I should get into med school and become a physician!

Even more pressure was applied to me because my uncles were established doctors themselves. To my impressionable young mind, they were the only ones purchasing new Cadillacs every couple of years, living in spacious homes and taking exotic vacations. No one had to put a gun to my head to make me want to stay on that path, even after giving my life to Jesus back in junior high. I still wanted everything that went along with that respectable profession, but I hadn't given any serious thought to how the Lord might want to use me as a physician.

Growing up in a Bible-teaching church, I don't recall anyone ever challenging me to rethink my vocational identity in light of passages that declare every Christian to be a minister and a missionary (1 Peter 2:9-10). Me, a priest of the King of kings, as well as a medical doctor? That unsettling combination is the exception for stellar Christians, not the rule for run-of-the-mill believers like me, right? Can't I still stay on whatever vocational path I desire, as long as I attend church regularly and tithe ten percent of my gross income? Or was that ten percent of my net income after taxes?

With this mindset I almost managed to make it all the way through college without ever questioning my lifelong plans to be some kind of doctor who also happened to believe in Jesus. But throughout my entire senior year and the year that followed graduation, I began to wrestle with the Lord over my true vocational identity. I first had to admit that my motives for wanting to be a doctor had very little to do with this being the way God could use me to do the "family business," helping to alleviate pain and suffering and offering real hope to others. I basically wanted to be a doctor so I could enjoy the prestige that typically surrounds that noble profession and so I could acquire the upscale lifestyle that was usually part of that same package. As I became more aware of the call of God on every Christian to serve his purposes, it began to dawn on me that whatever my profession or job, I primarily needed to see myself as Christ's holy servant.

As I studied the Bible with some close friends during my final two years in college, I started to face two critical truths. First, in spite of my confident assertions that I was going to be a doctor one day, I had no idea what I wanted to be when I grew up. Second, regardless of the career path(s) I would eventually select, God had already selected the vocational identity he wanted me to embrace: a minister and missionary of the Gospel.

The fact that God's Spirit eventually called me to become a local church pastor one year after graduating from college does not mean everyone is called to live out their priestly identity as a vocational pastor or a missionary. You may decide you want to be a doctor or a nurse or a locksmith or a stay-at-home parent, but *whatever* it is you choose, the Lord has first chosen us all to serve as Christ's royal priests in the world. Your "parish" may turn out to be a children's AIDS ward in Harlem or Bangkok. Or it might be among the rank and file in a giant factory. Or it might be within the elite circles of power in a global corporation. Or the Lord God might even be calling you to minister primarily at home, investing in your own family and in your neighbors' lives. What's most important is not what we do to earn a living but that we ultimately live, labor and love as Christ's ministers and missionaries, ever eager to serve God's purposes in the world and increasingly grateful that the Lord spared no expense to adopt us into his new family.

In so many ways, becoming a church pastor simplified coming to grips with what should be every Christian's identity as a priest of the King of kings. In retrospect, however, I should have been taught that this new identity came with being spiritually adopted long before I ever confessed my faith in Christ. Growing up in an American Baptist church, I do recall occasionally hearing that the church consisted of a priesthood of all believers, but the reality was that the pastor was supposed to be the only priest while the rest of us were simply lay people. We expected our pastors to exemplify Christ's qualities of unselfishness, sacrifice, devotion to the Father and clean living. So long as I did not believe that the Lord was calling me to be a pastor or a career missionary, I believed I was free to establish whatever identity I so desired. Even with those years of Sunday school classes, sermons and Bible studies, somehow I missed hearing that God the Father had adopted me as a full-fledged member of this new family in Christ so that I would follow in Jesus' footsteps. I had no idea that I'd been saved to serve in my Father's business of finding, caring for and adopting as many other spiritual orphans as possible.

Can you imagine the unleashing of life-giving, world-changing power that would occur if every one of us who professes to be following Jesus were convinced that we are, first and foremost, priests of the King? How many Christian doctors, dentists, optometrists or pharmacists would end up practicing their healing arts among those who can least afford it? How many Christian plastic surgeons would be repairing more facial disfigurements among the least of these instead of catering only to the vanities of the rich and famous? How many Christian families would be heavily invested in improving their public schools rather than holing up behind the walls of private Christian ones? What do you think Christian nutritionists would be doing with their skills if they truly believed they were ministers of Jesus? How much good do you think Christians who owned and ran their own companies could do if they looked at their employees through Jesus' eyes? What would CPAs or bankers do differently if they thought like ministers and missionaries of Jesus first? How would Christian teachers or janitors go about their work so others would start saying nicer things about Christians, and even the God of the Bible?

Imagine how the world would look; it would be more like the kingdom where God rules because all of us who believe would truly embrace this new identity as the core of who we now were in Christ. How would our churches be transformed if those of us in positions of influence started to lead in a way that reflected the diversity of God's forever family in Christ?

FINDING BROTHERS AND SISTERS WHERE YOU LEAST EXPECT IT

For the last decade, the Spirit of God has been challenging me to take my faith in Christ out beyond where I've grown comfortable, to a place where I can't rely on myself or my own practiced resources to get me through the hardships and setbacks. I've been led to choose a road less traveled where, if God truly did not show up and provide for us, we all would be utterly and hopelessly lost. One of those lonely roads is the one leading to the full recognition of all my adopted brothers and sisters in God's new family in Christ. This is something that probably won't come to pass during my lifetime, something that's uncomfortable and uncharted for everyone, but it's one thing that our common Father longs to see pursued passionately and with great determination.

Back in the mid-seventies, I took a step in the right direction by helping to establish one of the first ministries to English-speaking, Americanized Japanese and Chinese Americans—what was then an unusual combination. I had been told point-blank by a leading Chinese American pastor that I was thirty years too early, that Chinese churches in America were decades away from wanting to merge with their Japanese American spiritual brethren. But we persevered, intoxicated with the vision of creating a church where two groups that had long harbored historical animosities toward each other were tearing down the dividing walls and forging a new corporate identity in Christ. I was the first Chinese American to be called to the staff of this historically Japanese American church in 1981, a move calculated to send a clear message to the burgeoning numbers of ABCs (American-born Chinese) that this was truly becoming an Asian American church instead of simply a Japanese American church that was nice to Chinese Americans.

Making any paradigm shift stick always involves some painful choices. As we prepared to relocate from the barrio of East LA to the suburbs in the San Gabriel Valley in 1985, one of our most difficult decisions was whether to invite the tiny Japanese-speaking congregation across the street to come with us; some of the older members were the parents and grandparents of some of our members. Back in the 1950s, they had elected to become a separate church to be able to concentrate their energies on the Japanese-speaking population.

By 1985, the Japanese-speaking church had dwindled down to almost nothing, reflecting the demographic change of the formerly Japanese neighborhood. Since the 1950s, Evergreen Baptist Church of LA had also struggled with dwindling numbers, but it was nevertheless quite unique: a Japanese American church where English was the only official language. When the members called my predecessor—an Americanized Japanese American—to lead them, the modest church soon found that it could easily attract ABCs. My sister Melinda, her husband, Emery, and I were part of that early influx. The members warmly welcomed the rising waves of ABCs, and there came a point when it was clearly time to relocate and build a larger facility. But what about our brothers and sisters (actually, parents and grand-parents) across the street at the other church? After ten years of creating the niche for English-only, Asian American ministry, we labored over adding back a Japanese-speaking component with-out resurrecting issues we had left for dead since the 1950s. Wanting to be gracious, we ended up inviting them to come with us, but their pastor declined.

Although we felt like pioneers as we faced the challenge of rec-onciling this portion of Christ's family, admittedly what we were doing mirrored much of what was happening between the Chinese American and Japanese American communities without the intox-icating kiss of Christ's Spirit. Since the upheaval of the 1960s, these two distinct groups had been joining forces to increase their polit-ical visibility and power. Coming together in secular Asian Ameri-can clubs, caucuses and sports associations—wherever there were sufficient numbers—ABCs and *Sanseis* (third-generation Ameri-cans of Japanese descent) had already been forging friendships and marriages and families. Arguably then, we were addressing a demographic consolidation that was already occurring in secular society—and many ministries involving English-speaking Asian Americans are doing the same thing today.

Although the Asian American church and ministry movement is still in its childhood, as one of the pioneers, I view it now as more of a needed, natural evolutionary response to certain societal shifts than as a Spirit-intoxicated revolution to build radically redemptive and reconciled Christian communities beyond the barriers that society leaves in place. A priest-led revolution these days would be to establish Christ-centered, intentionally multiethnic churches where the dominant group is willing to give away power and privileges and where the marginal are beckoned to the center to be empowered and to influence corporate culture. That miracle will definitely not happen without God's inspiration, direction and correction. And it has a much better chance of happening if more of us feel completely secure in our place in God's family.

Since 1996, I've been so drunk with God's kisses that I have dedicated myself to forging a church where every member of my own extended family will feel loved, valued and respected. As of this writing there are twenty-one members in my extended family, and the following nine are not Chinese. My wife is Japanese American, and my two sisters-in-law are Southern White and Guamanian-Filipina, respectively. I also have a Korean niece, a White-Chinese niece and two Chinese-Guamanian-Filipina nieces. And the two boys that are carrying on our family name are White-Black and Chinese-Guamanian-Filipino.

In spite of the fact that we all love each other and the adults and older children are all Christians, it troubles me that most of these nine would not feel completely loved, respected and valued at most Asian American Christian gatherings. Tolerated and accepted? Probably. But celebrated and embraced? Doubtful. As my six non-Chinese nieces and nephews become teenagers or young adults, will they be welcomed at an Asian American Christian campus group or conference? For those that are partially Chinese, will their non-Chinese parts be recognized and celebrated, too? Sadly, at this point I seriously doubt it.

My very real experience of a loving, diverse extended family has awakened an intense desire to experience the same richness and closeness in my diverse extended family in Christ. I have a definite preference these days to address multiethnic Christian gatherings rather than Asian-specific ones. I am drawn to gatherings bent on fostering racial reconciliation. I am even reading more extensively now in order to expand my appreciation of multicultural issues.

Most of all, I have been casting a drunken vision before the members of the Evergreen Baptist Church of Los Angeles, one that is rooted in our Father's heart, written in his Word, and depicted in books like Acts and Revelation. While it has been uncomfortable at times, it has also been exhilarating to see the Spirit of Christ intoxicate more and more pre-loved children of God, not only with the hope stemming from their own adoptions but of belonging to an amazing new family that is multicultural, multilingual, multigenerational and even from different socioeconomic backgrounds. As of 2003, our church family now consists of about fourteen different Asian-Pacific Islander groups and ever-increasing numbers of Whites, Blacks, Latinos, multiethnic people and immigrants from all across the Pacific Rim.

Having such a heterogeneous congregation is certainly complicated and confusing. However, there are moments where our diversity makes it absolutely clear what we must do. The night following the terrorist attacks on the World Trade Center and the Pentagon, we held a special service. Our executive minister, Reverend Doctor Samuel Chetti, taught the biblical and historical roots of the Jewish-Arab enmity. Then our only Palestinian-Belgian member came to the microphone to share his family's story. He had spent many years in the West Bank and Gaza Strip regions and still had some family there. All of them were Christians, which startled many in attendance because the news media only reports about the Muslim Palestinians. His stories of struggling to apply God's unconditional love to his Jewish brethren and stories of his family's suffering disturbed the consciences of his fellow church members. His presence that night challenged our post-9/11 tendency to stereotype all Middle Eastern people as fanatical Muslim terrorists.

After his sharing I had planned to lay hands on Samir and pray for him, his family and his people. Caught up in the elixir of the moment, I instead summoned Larry, our Jewish American member, and Kathy, one of our Japanese American members who was only four when the government sent her family to a concentration camp in the aftermath of the attack on Pearl Harbor. When they placed their hands on Samir and began to love him with their prayers, it was as if Jesus was telling the fractured world that he alone had the power to bring true peace and unity. That was one of the most tangible experiences of the potent power resident in the complex family of Jesus.

Coming together as diverse fellow adoptees of God is truly wonderful and rare. Simply being together as a community in Christ can be a foretaste of heaven itself. But there is still so much to learn, so much blindness to uncover, so much pain to hear and heal. As one of my Latino American Christian brothers once wrote to me, "In a truly multiethnic [gathering], no one is comfortable."

It's much easier to surround ourselves with folks who resemble us, think like us, vote like us, live in similar neighborhoods and embrace the same theological paradigms. The unbelieving world hears our frequent claims of singing a new and different tune, but all it takes is one look at our homogeneous cliques and they dismissively say, "You're no different than us. You're singing the same old song you used to sing, the same one that we've always sung as we organize our secular clubs and circles of friends. The only difference is, we don't claim we're not doing it." Is it any wonder the world remains skeptical today, in spite of how we testify to the saving work of Jesus?

But there appears to be a growing number of intoxicated believers who are increasingly uncomfortable with maintaining the status quo of our faith families. As uncomfortable as change always is, Jesus is helping more of us feel at ease with singing Revelation's new song and marching together toward our inevitable shared future in heaven.

None of this can happen if we haven't individually experienced being embraced as fully adopted members of God's family. Realizing this, I am coming to accept that virtually every necessary and exciting thing that Jesus has put before our church—reconciling all of our people with each other; ministering to unwed moms, recovering drug addicts or at-risk youth—will take place only if and when each of the church's people is absolutely convinced of his or her secure place in God's family. And that's no small undertaking. It involves a major change of attitude, shifting from one that is ruled by rampant insecurity and anxiety to one that is marked by a quiet confidence rooted in the perfect and abundant love of Jesus. Until and unless this profound transformation occurs, all of our efforts toward reconciliation and reaching out are doomed to fail.

It has taken us close to six years to introduce a new song to our congregation, one that celebrates Jesus' heart for the marginalized, the overlooked and the unconvinced. Some have politely but firmly refused to sing with us. Others may look like they're singing along, but are only mouthing the words because they can't refute the song's redemptive premise. But part of the paradigm shift that goes along with this new song is the verse that emphasizes the amazing quality of the Father's love for every one of God's messy, messed-up adopted children.

Little by little, we're finally starting to see the evidence of a newly discovered confidence in our place in this complex family. We are learning how to bond with one another by discarding the masks that make us look so together and good when oftentimes we're not that at all. More of us are taking more chances with worshipful expressions of praise, fervent prayers and greater investments in the mission and ministries of this church. But we will most tangibly know God's people are feeling more secure in the full embrace of their heavenly Father when they are drunk enough to venture out beyond what's familiar and safe in order to love and serve others who are quite different from them.

One of our small groups, previously a comfortable neighborhood Bible study, recently threw a holiday party for women living in a home for recovering prostitutes and drug addicts. This group never would have done such a thing before. But God had been working on their fears and insecurities all these years through the guidance of their pastors and the counsel of God's Word. As a result of five years' worth of tiny, immeasurable inner transformations, they risked reaching out and fell head over heels in love with these courageous women. Now they're excitedly hatching plans to continue being involved in the women's lives. And since we believe that authentic reconciliation and mercy must flow from feeling that one's place in God's family is safe and secure, we have every reason to believe this ministry will flourish. Because if and when any of these women choose to join our church, a group of people will make sure they feel loved and valued.

Being adopted by loving parents is no guarantee that an adopted child will never worry about whether her parents ever regret choosing her to love as their own. If there's always a measure of doubt lurking in some portion of her mind, the adopted child might never feel free to open and enjoy this amazing gift of unsolicited love that comes with being a cherished and wanted member of a family.

Someone once shared with me how his parents, after having him, adopted his older brother. As young adults, he and his older sibling were marveling one day at how close they were. But when they boasted that they'd never fought as boys, their father quickly edited their flawed recollection. "You two used to really go at it. But don't you remember what happened that ended all your fighting? One day, you (the older adopted brother) were really giving it to your little brother. I pulled you off of him and grabbed you by both your shoulders. I looked you straight in the eye and said, 'You don't have to keep fighting for your place in this family. I already love you as much as I love your little brother. You are my son.' After that, you never fought with your little brother again."

From the look of things, many of us have never experienced our Father grabbing hold of us and telling us, once and for all, that we don't have to keep fighting for our place in God's family. Nearly my entire life and the bulk of my years as a Christian, I was not free to open and enjoy the unbelievable gift of God's grace. But the long and arduous journey of pre-loving the little girl that is now our daughter was my wake-up call from my Father. To paraphrase Jesus in Matthew 7:11, if I, even though I am an imperfect sinner, was more than willing to sacrifice and suffer to save and love a child into our family, how much more willing was our Father in heaven—who is love personified—to suffer and sacrifice to save and love a lost child like me and you.

If you dare to listen these days, God's people are singing the faint but distinct strains of a new song. It is a song that is learning to celebrate anew the undeniable first kiss of life from God as well as the intoxicating second kiss to new life in the Spirit. It is an outpouring of our own love for our heavenly Father and his only Son for pre-loving us enough to search for us and adopt us into a new and forever family. It is a song that resonates with the rhythms and stories of all its members. And more and more, it is a jubilant recognition that God still has more than enough love to adopt us and anoint us to join with him in pre-loving and finding more spiritual orphans who simply cannot imagine the new family that awaits them.

NOTES

Chapter 1: More Than Enough Love

[1] Leonard Sweet, *Post-modern Pilgrims: First Century Passion for the 21st Century World* (Nashville: Broadman & Holman, 2000), p. 8.

[2] William Klassen, "The Sacred Kiss in the New Testament," *New Testament Studies* 39 (1993): 134.

[3] Hugh Ross, *The Genesis Question: Scientific Advances and the Accuracy of Genesis* (Colorado Springs: NavPress, 2001), p. 19.

[4] John Ortberg, *Everybody's Normal Till You Get to Know Them* (Grand Rapids, Mich.: Zondervan, 2003), p. 39.

Chapter 2: To Be Made like God

[1] G. K. Chesterton, *Orthodoxy* (New York: Image Books, 1959), p. 60.

[2] Hugh Ross, *The Genesis Question: Scientific Advances and the Accuracy of Genesis* (Colorado Springs: NavPress, 2001), p. 54.

[3] Ibid., p. 55.

[4] Frederick Buechner, *Wishful Thinking: A Theological ABC* (San Francisco: Harper & Row, 1973), p. 40.

[5] Ibid., p. 98.

Chapter 5: Full and Forever Family Members

[1] Mike Yaconelli, *Messy Spirituality: God's Annoying Love for Imperfect People* (Grand Rapids, Mich.: Zondervan, 2002), p.17.

Chapter 6: Drunk with Kisses

[1] Leonard Sweet, *Post-modern Pilgrims: First Century Passion for the 21st Century World* (Nashville: Broadman & Holman, 2000), pp. 18-19.

[2] Ibid., p. 19.

Chapter 7: The Only One Worth Loving So Much

[1] *Exegetical Dictionary of the New Testament*, ed. Horst Balz and Gerhard Schneider (Grand Rapids, Mich.: Eerdmans, 1990), 1:130.

Ken Fong (M.Div., D.Min., Fuller) is senior pastor of Evergreen Baptist Church of Los Angeles, located in Rosemead, California. He has been a conference speaker throughout North America and at the Urbana Student Mission Convention. He has also served on the board of trustees for InterVarsity Christian Fellowship and Westmont College and as a contributing editor for *Leadership Journal*. He and his wife, Sharon ("Snoopy"), are the parents of their daughter, Janessa.